creative design

with your computer

Christopher Lumgair

GW00419704

TEACH YOURSELF BOOKS

For UK orders: please contact Bookpoint Ltd, 39 Milton Park, Abingdon, Oxon OX14 4TD. Telephone: (44) 01235 400414, Fax: (44) 01235 400454. Lines are open from 9.00 – 6.00, Monday to Saturday, with a 24 hour message answering service. Email address: orders@bookpoint.co.uk

For U.S.A. & Canada orders: please contact NTC/Contemporary Publishing, 4255 West Touhy Avenue, Lincolnwood, Illinois 60646 – 1975 U.S.A. Telephone: (847) 679 5500, Fax: (847) 679 2494.

Long renowned as the authoritative source of self-guided learning – with more than 30 million copies sold worldwide – the *Teach Yourself* series includes over 200 titles in the fields of languages, crafts, hobbies, sports, and other leisure activities.

A catalogue record for this title is available from The British Library.

Library of Congress Catalog Card Number: On file

First published in UK 1999 by Hodder Headline Plc, 338 Euston Road, London NW1 3BH

First published in US 1999 by NTC/Contemporary Publishing Company 4255 West Touhy Avenue, Lincolnwood (Chicago), Illinois 60646 – 1975 U.S.A.

Printed in Great Britain for Hodder & Stoughton Educational, a division of Hodder Headline Plc, 338 Euston Road, London NW1 3BH by Cox & Wyman Ltd, Reading, Berkshire.

Impression number	12	11	10	9	8	7	6	5	4	3	2	1
Year		2004	2003		2002	2001	2000	1999				

CONTENTS

Introduction   **1**

1 What is DTP?   **3**

Overview   3
    The birth of desktop publishing   3
    Production: then and now   4
Desktop publishing programs   7
    Page layout programs   7
    Draw programs   9
    Bitmap programs   10
Supporting technologies   12
    Graphics-based computers   12
    Page description languages   16
    PostScript and TrueType fonts   17
    ASCII and file formats   18
    Outputting devices   19

2 Choosing the right kit   **21**

Overview   21
Essential hardware   22
    Computers   22
    Monitors   23
    Input devices   24
    Output devices   27
Essential software   31
    Page layout programs   31
    Draw programs   33

Bitmap programs 35
Fonts 37

3 DTP in use 39

Overview 39
The DTP process 40
The overall process 40
The phases 40
Different uses of DTP 43
Case history 1 43
Case history 2 45
Case history 3 46
Case history 4 47
Case history 5 48

4 The creative desktop 50

Overview 50
Deciding on document formats 51
Page sizes 51
Folding methods 56
Binding methods 57
Permanent binding methods 58
Designing layouts 59
Defining grids 59
Page layout pointers 66
Working with typefaces 71
Typography 71
Typefaces 71
Classes of typefaces 72
Aspects of type 74
Serif and sans serif faces 76
Display faces 78
Script faces 78
Symbol faces 79
Working with faces and font sizes 79
Formatting type well 80
Aligning text 80
Spacing words and characters 82
Hyphenating text 85
Leading text 87
Tracking text 89
Spacing hierarchy 91

Aligning text to text   91
Defining paragraphs   95
Tabulating text   97
Emphasising words within text   100
Styling characters   102
Working with images   104
The role of images   104
Using off-the-shelf images   105
Using digital cameras   106
Creating informative diagrams   108
Digitising images   110
Obtaining good scans   111
Choosing image resolutions   114
Enhancing images   116
Removing noise and sharpening   118
Adjusting tones   120
Balancing colours   121
The colour wheel   122
Adjusting saturation   124
Cropping and cutting around images   124
Montaging and special effects   126
Ways of working with bitmapped images   128
Deciding on which file format to use   130
Using colour   133
What is colour?   133
Colour spaces explained   135
Working with colour spaces   137
Maintaining colour fidelity   138
Organising text   140
Text sources and copy editing   140
Preparing material on disk   141
Clearing text   142
Preparing indexes and glossaries   143
Hierarchy of information   145
On-screen editing   146
Points of style   149
Numbering systems   155

5 Volume printing

157

Pre-press and printing   157
Pre-press   159
Conventional printing   160

Digital press and 'print on demand'   163
Speciality printing   166
Papers and boards   168

Glossary   172

Index   177

INTRODUCTION

Desktop publishing has become the prime technology for producing printed communications the world over and probably, in the
not so distant future, it will become the *only* technology.

Many creative and craft disciplines are involved in its use and the
technologies employed in its operation are multiplying by the day.
All this can be a bit daunting to a newcomer to this subject.

It doesn't help that the term 'desktop publishing' refers both to a
swathe of digital technologies, nowadays embracing hypermedia in
addition to print, as well as to a broad creative discipline in its own
right. The wider, more ethereal, uses of DTP are not of our concern
but it is hoped that the role of technology and creativity in printed
communications are clarified in the following pages.

This book has several purposes: it aims to answer some of the
basic questions about desktop publishing: why and how did it start?
what is it? how does it work? what role does it play in the production
of printed documents?

It provides to newcomers an introduction to the key hardware
and software items essential for producing printed work of any sort.
The technologies are explained as simply as possible with crucial
features compared and guidance given, where appropriate.

It explains the production process in relation to printed work,
using several case histories to show DTP being successfully
employed in different types of organisations.

But mainly it gives guidance on getting professional-looking
results by suggesting areas for consideration, by covering accepted
conventions, by suggesting the best specification for type and
images and by alerting users to design pitfalls.

1

WHAT IS DTP?

This chapter covers:

● **the origins of desktop publishing**

● **three types of DTP program**

● **supporting technologies**

Overview

The birth of desktop publishing

The year 1985 witnessed the fusion of a combination of technologies known as 'desktop publishing' and marked the beginning of an era in printed communications, when people could for the first time produce printed publications from scratch and in their entirety on personal computers bought off-the-shelf.

In that year, an American company called Aldus launched on to the market a page layout program called PageMaker. Unique in concept, the program was written in a newly developed page description language called PostScript and it made use of two key Apple products, the Macintosh computer and the Laserwriter printer.

The genius behind PageMaker was Paul Brainard. Brainard was familiar with the sophisticated machines used to produce display advertisements for newspapers and he sought to produce a program with similar functions but at a much lower cost for those working in related fields.

Brainard chose the Macintosh computer because of its 'wysiwyg' display (what you see is what you get), its ability to handle graphics, fonts and colours and its unparalleled ease of use.

Apple not only had the only computer available at the time that could display high-definition graphics and fonts; since 1983 it had been working secretly on its Laserwriter, a monitorless computerised printer more powerful than the Macintosh itself. It was essentially a scaled-down version of the type of sophisticated photocopier-style computer printers used in large corporations and it produced exactly the print quality Brainard required.

Around this time Linotype, working in conjunction with Adobe, added PostScript interpreters to its high-end imagesetters. This provided the final link in the production process: the means to imageset DTP work as high-resolution films required by the printing industry.

Pagemaker turned out to be the key application which helped to give the Macintosh a reason for being; without the Macintosh, desktop publishing might still be an idea yet to be given form.

Many programs followed in PageMaker's wake: other page layout programs, such as QuarkXPress; paint programs, such as Painter; image processing programs, such as Photoshop, and draw programs, such as Illustrator and FreeHand, to name just a few.

Production: then and now

Then
Prior to the invention of desktop publishing, the production of most forms of printed matter required the participation of specialists in many fields, including graphic designers, copywriters, typists, paste-up artists, typesetters, reprographic technicians and printers (Fig. 1.1).

Each phase in the production process involved the use of different technologies, however small the job. Only specialists could operate equipment as it was only they who had the technical skills and knowhow.

Compositors within typesetting firms set text using sophisticated phototypesetting machines, paste-up artists in graphic art studios used large floor-standing cameras to size and prepare images for

desktop

publishing

technology

provides an

all-embracing,

multipurpose,

and integrated

creative and

production

environment

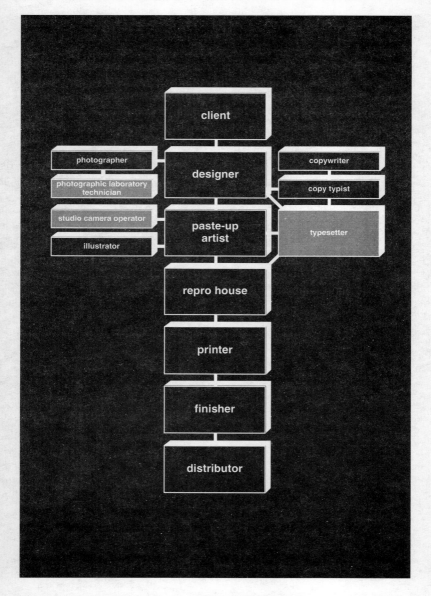

Fig. 1.1 Specialists involved in the traditional production process.
Those shown in grey panels are either made redundant by or absorbed into the
desktop publishing process

use on artwork, reprographic technicians at printing companies used scanners and other devices to scan photographs and copy artwork to create films for printing purposes, and so on.

These specialists often worked at different locations and for different organisations. The production of printed matter consequently involved a great deal of time-consuming communication and liaison to keep jobs on schedule and to ensure the accuracy of work.

Effectively, traditional practices distanced those directly responsible for projects from the production process.

Now

Desktop publishing ended all this by compressing the complete production cycle into the virtual reality of graphics-based computers. Instead of the involvement of different specialists working at different locations, printed matter could be produced by a single operator in one place. As a result, work could be done more cost effectively and within shorter timescales than was previously possible.

Instead of distancing people from the production process, desktop publishing empowered people to be much more closely involved, either by becoming part of a team of creative specialists working directly with DTP tools or by being the sole operator in charge of the whole process.

—— Desktop publishing programs ——

DTP programs can be divided into the following categories:

- page layout programs (some providing other facilities)
- draw programs (some providing other facilities)
- bitmap programs (for image editing and painting)

Page layout programs

Word processing, type composition, page layout, the integration of photographs and illustrations, printing; all these processes are integrated within a single working environment of page layout programs.

The programs in this category use the metaphor of the pasteboard, i.e. pages and adjacent pages are delineated within rectangular working areas representing the white boards used by paste-up artists working in the traditional manner (Fig. 1.2).

Pages appear within the pasteboards on the screen as they would look when printed. Pictures, graphics and fonts when added to the pages are shown in fine detail, in colour, to the right scale and in proportion.

Page layout programs describe pages mathematically using special page description languages (PDLs), Adobe's PostScript and Apple's QuickDraw GX being two such languages. Documents described by such languages don't contain images of page layouts. They are essentially text files containing written instructions on how the pages are constructed. They invariably include text, links to external picture files and sometimes include embedded photographs and illustrations.

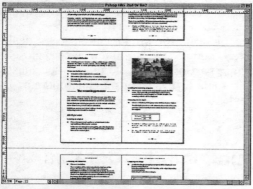

Fig. 1.2 An open QuarkXPress document showing two pages on the pasteboard

The beauty of using page description languages to describe DTP content is that everything on the pasteboard is a separate entity and can be altered at any time (Fig. 1.3). You can add, manipulate, move or delete items, such as text areas, picture areas, lines, etc. to your heart's content without affecting other items or leaving traces of your changes.

It's like working on a canvas with paint which never dries.

Key programs
QuarkXPress, Adobe PageMaker, Adobe FrameMaker

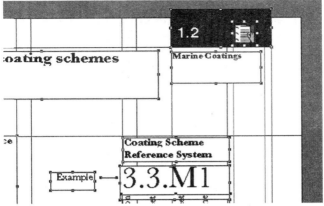

Fig. 1.3 A close-up of a page layout showing text and picture boxes

Draw programs

Draw programs provide an environment in which to illustrate, create graphic devices, such as logotypes, and to lay out pages.

Images created within draw programs are usually integrated into page layout documents – they become part of a host document's creative content. If a draw document's content is a page layout it's generally output (proofed, printed or imageset) from the draw program itself.

Draw, vector or object-orientated images as they are variously called comprise mathematically defined PostScript objects, each object representing a single entity within an illustration. Objects have a dimension and direction associated with them, as well as line widths (called strokes) and fill colours and/or patterns.

The objects are created within rectangular areas representing traditional artboards (Fig. 1.4). Often pages and printing areas are delineated within artboards in a similar way to how they are represented within page layout programs.

You can enter and format text in draw documents and incorporate bitmapped images. In some cases you can even manipulate the imported images or rasterise whole documents – convert them into bitmapped images – for further treatment within an image editing program.

Although the tendency is for vector images to look hard edged, the careful use of colour and gradients can give a soft air-brushed effect.

Complex modelling can be achieved in these programs by building forms from different objects and assigning suitable fills to the objects; the sides of a cone, for instance, could be built up from many triangular objects, each assigned a different gradient fill, giving a continuous tonal effect.

Draw objects are resolution free; they display and output at the resolution of the device involved. This means they always keep their sharpness when scaled, making them ideal for images intended to be used at many scales.

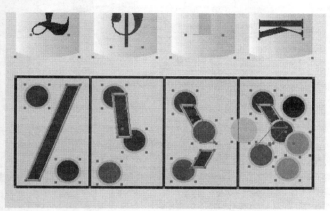

Fig. 1.4 A close-up of a draw image showing some objects

Key programs
Adobe Illustrator, Macromedia FreeHand, CorelDRAW!

Bitmap programs

Bitmap programs divide into two types: those which provide an environment in which to paint or illustrate – these are usually described as **paint programs** – and those which provide an environment in which scanning, retouching and image enhancement can take place – these are usually described as **image editing** or **image processing** programs.

Images scanned, created or modified within these programs are usually integrated into page layout or draw documents – they become part of their creative content.

A bitmapped, or raster image (from the German word *raster* meaning grid), can be described as a mosaic or canvas of pixels (picture elements), each pixel representing a single tone or colour (Fig. 1.5).

Whether pixels in an image are just black and white or one of a range of tones or colours is determined by an image's mode or bit-depth. The density of picture elements – an image's resolution – is measured in pixels per inch (ppi).

When you paint or edit bitmapped images, you are in fact just modifying pixel colours, however sophisticated a program's control. Within paint programs, the controls are mainly dedicated to simulating paint styles and media effects. In image editing programs, the controls are mainly dedicated to achieving photographic effects, distortions and montaging.

Rich modelling, simulated paint styles, colour-blends, montaging; all this can be achieved within bitmapped documents. However, a bitmapped image's resolution limits the amount it can be scaled without loss of sharpness and obvious degradation. Therefore, where possible, images which need to be used at many scales within host documents are originated within draw programs.

Fig. 1.5 A close-up of a bitmapped image showing its mosaic of pixels

---

Key programs
Paint: Fractal Design's Painter, Deneba's Canvas
Image editing: Adobe Photoshop, Live Picture, Macromedia xRes, Deneba's Canvas.

Supporting technologies

Graphics-based computers

Desktop publishing depends on key technologies, not least the presence of computer systems with strong graphical support, such as the Apple Macintosh and PCs equipped with Microsoft Windows.

Such systems have sophisticated, easy-to-use graphical user interfaces (GUIs), support 'wysiwyg' displays and have powerful colour and font handling capabilities.

In the early days the Macintosh was the only system with these attributes. Not surprisingly, Apple had the desktop publishing market to itself. Now PCs equipped with Windows offer users a credible alternative to the Macintosh for those working in PC-dominated work environments.

Easy 'point and click' control

Both the Macintosh and Windows systems employ iconic graphical interfaces controlled by means of a pointing device and keyboard (Fig. 1.6). Items such as storage devices, folders, documents and programs are represented by icons which when clicked or double clicked are activated or opened, depending on their function.

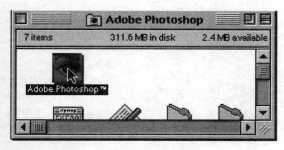

Fig. 1.6 Clickable icons within a window

Programs are controlled by selecting menu commands, buttons and check-boxes, often located within movable palettes and panels (called dialog boxes).

There is no need therefore to learn complicated programming languages to either operate the computers or to perform DTP tasks.

Programs with a consistent interface

Programs on both systems conform to strict interface standards and share common functions. For instance, the New, Open and Save commands in programs are always located in the same menu, have a consistent appearance and work in the same way. This means that once you have learnt the essentials of one program, you will immediately be able at least to find your way around another program without resorting to a manual.

A desktop large enough for the most expansive user

Both systems use the metaphor of a desktop, a virtual two-dimensional space where disk drives and other key items reside and over which windows are displayed.

Windows give a view into drives (hard, floppy discs, CD ROMs etc.), folders (the sub-divisions of drives) and documents (the files you work on). They are resizable, scrollable and can be overlapped, allowing the contents of more than one to be viewed at any one time (Fig. 1.7). This is particularly useful when you are working on a project involving many documents.

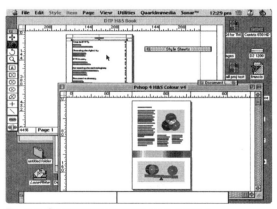

Fig. 1.7 Overlapping windows on a desktop

The desktop extends well past the edges of most monitor screens. In fact it's big enough to run across several screens should you have more than one monitor attached to your computer. Using multiple monitors gets around the fixed proportions and limited size of monitor screens. You can, for example, display palettes on one monitor, keeping the companion monitor free for document windows.

Text and graphics show as they will print

The high-resolution monitor screens used for DTP work are described as being 'wysiwyg' (what you see is what you get), i.e. they display text and pictures nearly as accurately as on the finished printed article.

DTP content is represented as pixels on the screen, whether the actual files are bitmapped or not. Letter forms are bitmapped to match dot for dot the typeface, size and style of a font you've chosen.

Special software routines are responsible for taking data from document files and fonts to draw the on-screen image, constantly updating it as you work.

You can therefore confidently manipulate your work on-screen at your pace, knowing that the integrity of the document you create will be maintained when printed.

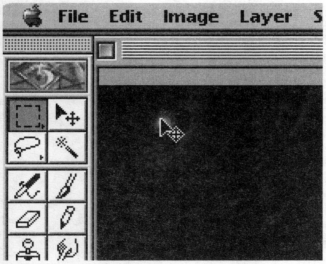

Fig. 1.8 Close-up of a monitor screen

Realistic representation of tones and colours

Monitor screens for DTP use are said to be bitmapped as each screen pixel is controlled by a bit or a series of bits in the computer's random access memory (RAM). These bits determine the colour of individual pixels and, consequently, the overall screen image (Fig. 1.8).

The pixels are pitched close enough together that when seen at more than a few inches away, the eye merges them together to give the sensation of continuous tones and colours. Even the smallest fonts can be displayed with reasonable fidelity at such a fine resolution.

The first Macintosh screen had a resolution of 72 pixels per inch (ppi) to match a unit of measure called a point in typography – Apple quite rightly thought that if a point was a small enough measure for font cutters, it would surely be a suitable resolution for monitors displaying graphics. In fact, most current monitor screens offer a choice of resolutions, some well in excess of this original specification.

More colours than you could ever possibly use

Colour is an important ingredient of most printed communications so it's not surprising that both systems have been designed with full colour support.

Most monitors can display millions of colours, provided they have the right level of video support. The number of colours a monitor can display at any one time is governed by its colour setting. Monitors can be set to display just two colours (black and white), 256 system colours, or thousands or millions of colours.

You can theoretically specify any one of 280 trillion colours within a DTP document, more than most video cards can display and certainly much more than the human eye can differentiate.

Colours chosen using digital palettes

Colours are specified within DTP programs using colour palettes or other controls, and in some cases by accessing the system's own colour picker. Colour monitors are essential for this task; indeed they are essential when working with any form of colour imagery.

Colours are defined in a number of ways:

- by mixing red, green and blue in various proportions (using the RGB colour space)
- by mixing cyan, magenta, yellow and black in various proportions (using the CMYK colour space)
- by selecting standard colours from a proprietary colour system, such as the Pantone Matching System (ink colours for illustrations, type and items in layouts are usually specified by this means)

Accurate and consistent colour across all devices

Colour is displayed accurately and consistently on-screen through the use of special colour management profiles which tap into Apple's underlying ColorSync 2 technology.

ColorSync 2 is installed as standard on Macintoshes. On the Macintosh the profiles conform to ICC standards (International Colour Consortium), whilst on the PC they conform to compatible ICM standards (Image Colour Management).

These profiles manage colour across all devices used in the DTP workflow whatever system is being used, including scanners, monitors, digital printers and printing presses.

Page description languages

You will be aware by now of the crucial role page description languages (PDLs) play throughout the desktop publishing process. To begin with, page layout documents are written in such languages.

When you choose commands in a page layout program, special code is automatically written describing the changes you are making. You are not aware of this whilst you are working and may not ever see the instructions unless you open a file using a word processor.

```
grestore}{pop}ifelse}bdf4/sgt{2 copy
known{get true}{pop pop
false}ifelse}bdfN/kif{currentfont
dup/FontMatrix get exch/FontInfo
sgt{true}{currentfont/df sgtX{dup/FontInfo
```

Fig. 1.9 A glimpse into a PostScript file

Proprietary software routines, such as QuickDraw on the Macintosh, continually interpret the coded instructions to provide an on-screen image so you can see what you are doing. To enable you to output documents, the same imaging systems are employed within printing devices.

Whilst one or two page layout and draw programs in the past employed Apple's QuickDraw GX PDL, in the main documents nowadays are written in PostScript (Fig. 1.9). Such documents, in theory, can be output on QuickDraw GX devices, but since most

DTP users have printers with PostScript interpreters, proprietary imaging routines, such as QuickDraw, are often bypassed.

An important aspect of PostScript is that it's device-independent, i.e. its technology is not restricted to certain machines. This is a great benefit as documents can be output on successive devices for different purposes without any re-specification. It's quite normal to proof on desktop printers – maybe on both grayscale and colour devices – and later to output pages on high-resolution imagesetters at a bureau.

PostScript and TrueType fonts

Page description languages not only describe page layouts and illustrations, they are especially powerful in generating fonts both for the screen and for printing.

Individual letter forms are stored as outlines which can be scaled to any size without loss of definition. Outline fonts using TrueImage (QuickDraw) technology are called TrueType and those using PostScript technology Adobe Type 1. PostScript fonts for historical reasons come in both outline (Fig. 1.10) and bitmapped form. Originally the bitmaps were used solely for screen display at certain fixed text sizes.

Fig. 1.10 An outline font: how it's constructed, how it looks on-screen and how it looks when printed

Nowadays most people use a program called Adobe Type Manager (ATM) which automatically rasterises (bitmaps) the outline fonts to the resolution of the monitor screen. This means that PostScript fonts are sharp whatever their point size.

TrueType and PostScript fonts are available in a very wide range of typefaces, in both Windows and Macintosh versions. Custom designs can be created within dedicated programs, such as Macromedia Fontographer.

ASCII and file formats

Standardising the representation of text

Although this section is primarily about supporting technologies, I include a mention of ASCII here because of its crucial role in standardising the representation of letters, numbers, symbols and controls.

ASCII (American Standard Code for Information Interchange) provides the necessary standardisation between programs to enable you to copy text between files and to transfer files between computers and computer systems with the minimum of fuss.

Each of 256 characters and symbols potentially accessible on computer keyboards is represented by a number from 0 to 255. When you type the capital letter A, for example, it's represented by the character 65, which is coded in binary form. So text within document files is recorded as a series of numbers representing the characters you typed.

File formats

Documents containing plain ASCII text are saved as ASCII files which can be opened or imported into most DTP programs.

DTP documents themselves, however, can't be saved in this manner as they make use of character codes to define the appearance and style of their text – their formatting. The coded characters unfortunately don't conform to any internationally agreed standard; they vary from program to program.

Because of this, the documents are saved in special file formats which differentiate between both text and formatting code. Some of these formats are unique to the programs which created them; others not so. Provided such files are opened or accessed by a program which understands their code – usually only the originating program but not always – any text will be correctly formatted.

The same principle applies to picture file formats; TIFFs, for example, can be opened by many image processing programs (as they are a de facto standard), whereas Photoshop 5 file format can only be opened successfully by the Photoshop 5 application program.

Documents you can view and print anywhere

Because clients wishing to view or print out DTP documents often lack the originating host program, special programs have been developed to create portable documents to cater for their needs. Documents saved in Portable Document Format (PDF) show layouts with fonts, bitmapped and vector images imaged with total accuracy. Comments can be added to the files but they normally can't be edited – to do this you still need the creator programs.

PDFs are also used to streamline the outputting of files. By distilling unwieldy PostScript code, PDF files are not only much more compact than their source files, they are also device-independent. This means that only one version of a single file is required for outputting to different devices, e.g. you can use the same single file, in turn, to output to a proofing device, digital press and conventional press.

Outputting devices

Apple's first Laserwriter with its 300 dots per inch (dpi) processor and Canon print engine provided the model for all future DTP outputting devices. Instead of exclusively accepting Apple's QuickDraw routines, it had a PostScript interpreter and resident PostScript fonts (the latter using designs from the International Typeface Corporation).

Today there's a wide choice of marking technologies available including laser, inkjet, dye-sublimation and thermal wax transfer. Each technology has its unique print characteristics and is suited to a particular task. Many of these devices output at 600 dpi or more, print in both grayscale or colour, and have resident TrueType fonts. Some of them give near-typeset quality text whilst others give photorealistic results barely distinguishable from photographic prints.

The way these devices work is as follows: document instructions and linked data are sent from computer to printer. The instructions are intercepted and read by an interpreter – usually PostScript – which constructs an image of each document page.

Each page image is then bitmapped (turned into a grid of dots) by a raster image processor (RIP for short). The bitmapped image is then transferred directly or indirectly to the surface of paper (or other substrate) by one of the marking technologies mentioned above. If colour is employed, the bitmapping process is repeated for each ink colour.

Film output for non-digital volume printing is provided by 'high-end' PostScript imagesetters, developed from devices originally designed solely to output type. Nowadays such devices are designed from the ground up for DTP output. They work in a similar manner to other printing devices but print only in black and at very high resolutions (usually 1270 dpi or more).

2

CHOOSING THE
RIGHT KIT

This chapter covers:

- essential hardware devices
- essential software programs

Overview

In this chapter I survey some of the items of hardware and software essential to the design and production of printed documents.

The survey is not intended to be comprehensive nor can it be as it would require a whole book to do the subject justice. In fact it is very selective, leaving out many items which may be useful for certain specialised tasks but which are not strictly necessary for general desktop publishing work.

Because new technologies and products are being developed the whole time, I have intentionally not gone into too much detail either, particularly in regard to software programs, as their detail specifications are prone to frequent change, more so than any other type of product.

——————— Essential hardware ———————

Computers

Most graphics-based computers – Apple Macintoshes and PCs equipped with Microsoft Windows – are suitable for DTP use. Of course, a lot depends on the availability of programs for a particular system. Unix systems are probably the least supported in this regard.

When choosing a computer, several factors need to be taken into consideration. Firstly, which system should one choose – Apple Macintosh or Microsoft Windows? There is no doubt that the ease of use and elegance of the Apple Macintosh interface makes it a firm favourite with owner-users but other considerations need to be taken into account (Fig. 2.1).

If you are planning to work in a PC environment (an office full of networked PCs), it may be more practical to fit in with the current regime as internal technical support will not usually extend to Apple products and you may encounter file format compatibility problems.

Fig. 2.1 Power Macintosh G3 from Apple

If you are working in a home office, it's usually best to choose a system used by others in your line of business, e.g. if you are a freelance graphic designer and you work with design companies you would probably be best advised to choose from Apple products which dominate this market.

Certainly bureaus at present prefer outputting files from Apple Macintoshes but this situation will change, as more and more DTP work is being generated on PCs.

Then there is the computer's specification to be taken into account. Computers are usually described in terms of processor speed, which is measured in megahertz (MHz), volatile memory or RAM, which is measured in megabyte (MB) and disk storage space, which is often measured in gigabyte (GB).

Nowadays most new machines incorporate the Intel Pentium processor or, in the case of Apple Macintoshes, the Motorola PowerPC processor. Most run at well over 200 MHz, fast enough for most programs, including processor-intensive image editing programs.

Most machines come with 24 MB of RAM as standard which is adequate for most work but probably too low for running programs concurrently and for heavy-duty image editing work. Anything from 48 MB upwards is more appropriate for this pattern and level of work.

Internal hard drives should ideally be at least 500 MB. This sounds large but they need to provide enough room for bloated operating systems, increasingly large DTP programs, a large number of fonts and quite possibly huge bitmapped images, created by scanning.

In addition to the above an internal CD drive is essential – for loading programs, fonts and library images – and an internal Zip drive, or other large-capacity ejectable drive, is desirable – for transferring files larger than 1.5 MB to bureaus.

Monitors

Ideally monitors for DTP work should be large. Unless you are just working on small-scale documents, screen sizes should be at least 17 inches (measured diagonally). Screens this size display two A4 pages side by side at approximately two-thirds full size, subject to the screen resolution setting.

If neither money, space nor weight is a problem, 20 or 21 inch screens are preferable. With these screens the same work can be viewed in its entirety at nearly life size.

Most monitors use cathode-ray tube technology which is both extremely heavy and bulky. Fortunately, for those with little space or physical strength, newer flat-screen technologies are already on the market. They are light and compact and, as prices come down, they offer a solution to weight-conscious users who wish to have large screens without the currently associated problems.

The colour support provided by the computer should be 16-bit or higher at a high screen resolution. Less than 16-bit gives dithered colours which are not accurate enough and have an unsightly patterned appearance.

Input devices

Scanners

Scanners used for DTP work are usually either flatbed or dedicated transparency units. Both types employ state-of-the-art CCD technology.

Flatbed scanners are mostly of the reflective type. They are designed to scan flat items, such as artworks and prints. Some are also transmissive to enable them to scan transparencies. Dedicated transparency scanners are solely transmissive. They are designed to scan transparencies of one or more standard formats.

A few of the more expensive flatbed scanners are able to scan transparencies well enough for production purposes. Multi-format transparency scanners also give production quality but they come with a high price tag. However 35 mm scanners are a less expensive option.

A scanner's optical resolution needs to be adequate for the work you wish to do. Resolution is described as either optical or optical supplemented by interpolated; interpolation is used to resample optically recorded data during the scanning process.

Some scanners are described as having two optical resolutions, such as 300–400 ppi (dpi). The lower figure represents the number of CCD elements across the scanner bed, the higher figure represents the number of recorded steps the CCD takes to pass down the length of the bed. The lower figure, in this case 300, is invariably interpolated to match the higher figure, in this case 400. This gives a better result than an optical resolution of 300 in both directions.

A scanner needs to support 24-bit colour or above. This will enable you to scan in full colour (recording over 16 million colours) as well as in grayscale and line. Bit depths higher than 24-bit are better able to record details in the darkest and lightest areas of a subject.

Here are some factors which need to be taken into consideration:

- the type of subjects you propose to scan
- a scanner's ability to record colour accurately
- a scanner's ability to record sufficient detail in highlight and shadow areas
- a scanner's ability to control noise and avoid ghosting in shadow areas
- a scanner's preview size
- a scanner's general ease of use
- a scanner's software features, e.g. whether you can rotate or de-screen images
- the manufacturer's backup support
- the quality of a scanner's user manuals
- your budget

Flatbed scanners are available from Agfa, Dianippon, Epson and Linotype Hell. Transparency scanners are available from Kodak, Nikon, Microtek and Polaroid.

Cameras

Digital cameras fall into three categories: low end, mid-range and professional. Since low-end devices are more suited to multimedia and web applications and professional cameras are the preserve of the specialist photographer, I will restrict my discussion to mid-range products (Fig. 2.2).

Most cameras in this category use a CCD (charge-coupled device), a light-sensitive chip used for image gathering. It acts in a similar way to film in a traditional camera, with images recorded according to the level of light falling on the camera's sensors. Colour images are achieved by placing the CCD behind coloured filters, so that each adjacent sensor registers one of three colours, red, green and blue. The results are combined to create a single full-colour pixel. Some cameras are beginning to use CMOS chips, which are theoretically superior in performance but they are currently suffering teething problems.

Whilst mid-range cameras are improving all the time, storage capacity and image quality are still wanting to some degree.

Memory chips need to be capacious so that one does not have to constantly upload images to a computer during shooting. Storage types currently vary from 4 MB internal flash memories, which are fast, to standard floppy disks, which are creaky.

Optical resolutions need to be relatively high otherwise image definition will be compromised.

Mid-range cameras tend to give resolutions of anything from as low as 640×480 pixels to as high as 1152×864. Assuming a production resolution of 300 ppi (dpi), the latter matrix of 1152×864 pixels would give optimum image dimensions of 9.75×7.32 mm. Subsequent enlargement may lead to loss of image definition and pixelation.

Fig. 2.2 Epson's PhotoPC 700 digital camera

The resolution or resolving power of digital cameras is also determined by the quality of their lenses. Lenses designed for conventional cameras are often unsuitable for medium-resolution digital work as the smallest detail these lenses can resolve is often less than the sensors can theoretically record.

Digital cameras on the market include those developed by established photographic companies – Agfa, Fuji, Kodak – and computer imaging companies such as Epson.

Here are some factors which need to be taken into consideration:

- imaging speed – number of photographs per minute
- optical resolution
- colour depth, such as 24-bit
- colour accuracy
- ease of uploading to computer
- sharpness of image
- performance of LCD viewing screen
- built-in flashlight/zoom lens
- a camera's general ease of use
- the manufacturer's backup support
- the quality of a camera's documentation and user manuals
- your budget

Other input devices

There are many other input devices available to the DTP operator including such items as graphics tablets (pressure sensitive pads equipped with pens), hand-held scanners, trackballs (essentially stationary up-side-down mice) and 'ergonomic' keyboards.

Certainly a graphics tablet is essential for drawing work if line variation is required and hand-held scanners can be useful for scanning images for reference purposes. As regards the other two items, neither can be regarded as essential but some users prefer them to the standard items normally supplied with computers.

Output devices

Low-volume printing devices

Many types of marking technology are used to output DTP work, including inkjet, thermal wax transfer, laser and dye-sublimation.

Inkjet printers come in both desktop and large format, floor-standing models. Some employ Canon's bubblejet technology whilst others are based on Epson's more recently developed MicroPiezo technology. Both types tend to be fairly low cost and lacking PostScript.

MicroPiezo generated prints have a much higher resolution than those generated by a bubble jet (1440 dpi as opposed to 720 dpi); as a consequence they are less prone to banding in gradient areas. Their colours are much more accurate than those achieved by bubble jet and because of their method of operation their prints don't suffer from ink splattering or paper cockling. The latter problem can be minimised on Canon's system by using suitably coated substrates.

The lack of PostScript rules out both types for serious DTP work unless a software RIP is used to rasterise output. However large-format versions designed for medium-run poster production tend to have built-in PostScript and their printed output is certainly good enough for their intended applications.

In a bubblejet printer tiny droplets of ink are squirted onto paper. Microscopic nozzles are first filled with ink. An electric current heats the nozzles rapidly causing the ink in the nozzles to be flash-boiled. The resulting bubbles expand and force a tiny droplet of ink out onto the paper. The current is switched off, the nozzles cool, the bubbles collapse and the resulting vacuum sucks more ink into the nozzles. This process repeats itself many thousands of times a second.

I explain how the MicroPiezo system works when discussing high-end versions used for proofing – see later in this chapter.

Thermal wax transfer printers are fairly inexpensive but like inkjet printers they tend not to be PostScript. They can print quite vibrant colours but are poor at rendering type. They tend to be used for creating overhead transparencies or for printing on-off colour pages.

In a thermal wax printer a roll of foil is loaded containing each of the four process colours in page-sized chunks. In the printing process each of the sections of foil is heat-sealed to the paper or film surface in the appropriate areas, building up a full-colour image.

Laser printers are available at both low and medium price levels. They are relatively fast and their print quality is generally quite good, equivalent to colour photocopies – not surprisingly, since they use the same basic technology. Laser prints are good enough for business documents and for design 'roughs' but they do not render colours accurately enough for final design visuals.

In a laser printer particles of toner are electrostatically given a negative charge: meanwhile a laser picks out the image of a page onto a photosensitive drum, and the dots on the drum which make up the image are positively charged. The toner adheres to the positive dots, which get transferred to a rubber belt and then onto the paper surface, where heat is used to fix the toner. In a colour printer this process is repeated four times – once for each of the four process colours.

Dye-sublimation printers give very high-quality results, hardly distinguishable from traditional photographic colour prints, but they are expensive both to purchase and to operate and are very slow. As a consequence they are mainly used for outputting photo montages and other one-off images. I explain how this system works when discussing high-end versions used for proofing – see later in this chapter.

Most of the printing devices discussed output colour as halftone dots. The eye merges the cyan, magenta, yellow and black dots together to give the illusion of continuous tone; dye-sublimation printers output colour as continuous tone by fusing or blending the process colours together. Some can print in both ways. Certainly colours generally tend to look better printed as continuous tone but not type and linear work.

Choosing the right printer is perhaps easier than choosing the right scanner as it's much easier to compare results.

Here are some factors which need to be taken into consideration:

- printing speed – number of copies per minute
- choice of substrate and finish
- output resolution
- cost per print
- colour accuracy
- built-in Ethernet
- sharpness of type
- general ease of use
- manufacturer's maintenance backup support
- quality of a printer's documentation and user manuals
- your budget

Proofing devices

Proofers, basically high-end printers used solely to output documents for quality control purposes, fall into one of two basic types: they are either digital systems or from-film systems.

Digital systems generate proofs directly from a DTP file whereas from-film proofs are created from film separations. Digital proofs are quicker to process, require less consumables, such as paper and inks, and are thus less costly on a per print basis than 'from-film' proofs.

Two types of technologies dominate digital proofing: dye-sublimation and inkjet. Both are benefiting from continual technical development and maturing colour calibration systems so their output quality is improving year by year.

Dye-sublimation proofing

Dye-sublimation proofing involves the use of gases applied from a roll of dye-impregnated film onto special paper. The roll is made up of cyan, magenta, yellow and black dyed sheets joined in sequence. As the paper is passed through the printer, a heating element behind the paper causes the dye within to 'sublimate' – to change from dye to gas without liquefying first. The process transfers to paper tiny diffused areas of gas rather than halftone dots, giving a continuous tone as you expect to see in a photograph.

One advantage of this type of proofing is that proofs don't suffer from arbitrary half-tone screening, i.e. screen angles and pitches which differ from final film output. Another is that spot colours can be printed, including both fluorescents and metallics (subject to model type).

However, the technology does not reproduce small text well nor is it able to reproduce all the properties of the final offset-litho print. Since it can't reproduce dots, it won't alert you to potential moiré patterns.

Products using this type of proofing include the Imation Rainbow, Agfa-Gevaert DuoProof, Tektronix Phaser, Seiko Instruments SII ColorPoint and the NewGen ChromaxPro.

Inkjet proofing

One type of inkjet proofing system is termed MicroPiezo and was developed by Epson. The system involves propelling tiny droplets of ink onto the surface of paper. Ink is drawn from tanks in the body of the printer and precisely positioned onto the paper surface by the action of vibrating Piezo crystals. These crystals vibrate at fixed frequencies when an electric current is applied to them. This property is known as the piezo effect (from the ancient Greek 'piezein' meaning 'to press'). The crystals, located in the print head, are essentially miniature pumps and the colour accuracy and level of detail they achieve is of a high order.

Inkjet systems which employ a halftone screen give a closer match in terms of detail to the final offset-litho print than dye-sublimation proofs. Dot gain can be matched to final output and any moiré patterns and other halftone defects show up and can be addressed before going to press. Also type is reproduced considerably sharper than on dye-sublimation proofs. However overall quality, in terms of colour accuracy, is slightly inferior to that achieved by dye-sublimation.

Products using inkjet systems for proofing include the Scitex Iris, Dupont Digital Cromalin and Epson Proofer.

From-film proofing

From-film proofs – sometimes called analogue or off-press proofs – work by taking data from film separations which have been output from an imagesetter. They are much more expensive to produce than digital systems, being more labour intensive to process and requiring the outputting of film positives, which in themselves are expensive.

Various methods are used to create from-film proofs. I explain the overlay method here. One of the four CMYK films is pressed against an overlay sheet which is then exposed to light. The overlay sheet is pressed against a substrate which is softened in the image areas. Coloured powder is then applied to the substrate, adhering only to the soft areas. The process is repeated for each film, using new overlay sheets against the same substrate sheet.

The main advantage of from-film proofs is that they are a step closer than digital proofs to a conventional printing press. Being made from the very films that are planned to be used to image the printing plates, they are the next best thing to wet proofs – proofs actually made on a printing press. Any problems with films will show up including those associated with moiré patterns, registration and such like.

Products using this type of system include Cromalin and Matchprint.

Essential software

Page layout programs

QuarkXPress and PageMaker

QuarkXPress and Adobe PageMaker between them dominate the page layout market. At the time of writing QuarkXPress is certainly perceived as the industry standard with PageMaker a close second (Fig. 2.3).

Choosing between these two products can be difficult as they are equally powerful and have many features in common. Furthermore the capabilities of both products can be extended indefinitely using third-party programs (called XTensions in QuarkXPress and Plug-ins in PageMaker).

There is no doubt that QuarkXPress has the superior method for defining text areas – text is contained within boxes rather than sitting directly on the page – and the recent addition of bézier drawing tools and clipping controls has given the program a further enhancement, obviating the need to use separate draw and image processing programs for key tasks. All this should be set against the benefits accruing from PageMaker's close links with Adobe's other publishing programs.

Both programs support ICC colour profiles and Hexachrome colour and both feature multiple master pages, a spell checker, a search and replace function, grouping and locking controls, and trapping controls.

Fig. 2.3 QuarkXPress is the predominant page layout program

The decision comes down to a choice between the leading product in the field preferred by all those involved in the outputting of files for print or instead a very capable product which is an integrated part of a wider publishing collection.

Main differences between QuarkPress and PageMaker:

	QuarkXPress	*PageMaker*
Character-based stylesheets	•	
Open Press interface	•	
Layers		•
Object masking		•
Imposition	•	
Table editor		•
Clipping paths	•	
Bézier tool	•	
Save page as EPS	•	

FrameMaker

FrameMaker is a much less widely used product. It's the preferred choice for producing long and complex documentation, such as manuals. Automatic formatting controls cover not just type but layouts, which are governed by a series of style and behaviour rules. It's a complex program to master, requiring a logical and procedural mind-set and as such it's less suited to general publishing applications.

See also FreeHand, CorelDRAW! and Canvas under Draw programs.

Draw programs

Adobe Illustrator, Macromedia FreeHand and CorelDRAW! between them dominate the draw market. Illustrator and FreeHand are widely used in publishing and design fields where the Apple Macintosh predominates, whilst CorelDRAW! has a very strong presence (over 80% market share) within commerce and industry, as it was one of the only draw programs available on the Windows system for many years.

All three are excellent all-rounders yet each has unique features, which explains why most designers end up using more than one. This is certainly true of Illustrator and FreeHand users.

Illustrator

Illustrator has a similar interface to Photoshop – which reduces the learning curve for existing Photoshop users. It employs a pasteboard metaphor. You create your illustration within a pasteboard whose size you can specify.

It has good colour controls and allows you to create multi-coloured gradients and repeat patterns. If you don't have Photoshop you can even use Photoshop plug-ins to alter imported bitmapped images, albeit at a slower rate than if you apply filters within Photoshop itself.

Its many other features include an excellent graph-making tool which lets you import data from spread sheets, filters which automate the combining of separate objects and rasterising controls.

It has superb colour controls and both ColorSync and ICC profiles are supported for accurate colour matching and output.

You can import a wide variety of file formats into Illustrator documents and the program supports Apple's Publish and Subscribe for the automatic updating of amended files.

FreeHand

Macromedia FreeHand (Fig 2.4) is a worthy competitor to Illustrator. It's easier to use yet has an equally good if not better set of features. It employs a page metaphor which means that it can be truly regarded as a combined draw and page layout program. You create your illustration or illustrations within pages whose sizes you can specify.

It has an excellent inspector palette which brings together many functions. Its pointer tool allows direct rescaling and basic object manipulation.

Its colour controls are as good as Illustrator's and it similarly supports both ColorSync and ICC profiles.

As with Illustrator you can import a wide variety of file formats into FreeHand documents and let Apple's Publish and Subscribe automatically update amended files.

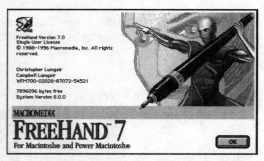

Fig. 2.4 FreeHand, probably the best draw program

CorelDRAW!

CorelDRAW! is a combined draw, bitmap and page layout program. It has a vast range of tools, perhaps more than in any competitor program, and many built-in functions which in FreeHand and Illustrator would probably be treated as plug-ins. This gives it a daunting interface which is both complex to use and difficult to customise.

Its sophisticated style sheet and object 'preset' features, however, are both well designed and ensure consistency within documents whilst enhancing productivity. Some of its features are only found in product and architectural design programs; dimension line drawing is automated, there's a palette for storing symbols and a bundled program for the photo-realistic rendering of objects.

Its painting features include an interactive brush, live lenses for simulating overlayed tints, a two-pane preview for viewing before and after effects and a mesh warp tool for grid based distortions.

Canvas

Whilst Deneba's Canvas strength lies in its drawing features, it's really a hybrid program in which one can draw, paint as well as layout pages. For drawing it has a comprehensive range of tools, including a very impressive 3D tool which enables object profiles to be extruded. Its dimensioning tool provides ways to append object and document specifications as in programs used for product and architectural design.

It has the equivalent to Illustrator's Pathfinder and FreeHand's Xtras filters to automate the merging, subtracting, mixing and over-lapping of objects. Its image editing capabilities are similar to Photoshop but not as comprehensive and its page layout approach is closer to PageMaker than to QuarkXPress.

Bitmap programs

Painter

Fractal Design's Painter is the leading 'natural-media' painting pro-gram despite it being slow in operation and having an awkward, dif-ficult-to-learn interface. It has over 100 brush tools for retouching photographs, applying textures, distortion work and 'natural-media' painting. The painting tools let you work with such media as oils, watercolours and pastels without ever getting your hands dirty.

Its files are fully interchangeable with Photoshop, allowing images to be transferred from one environment to the other without losing mask, channel and path information. It has 'dynamic floaters' which work in a similar manner to Photoshop's layer palette, allow-ing modifiable special effects to be applied such as burnt paper and kaleidoscopes. It supports CMYK mode as well as Hexachrome.

Photoshop

Adobe Photoshop (Fig. 2.5) is undoubtedly the most powerful and flexible image editing program around. It has the widest set of fea-tures of any program in its class and they are well laid out and easy to use. It's a veritable 'Swiss army knife' as it can manipulate images in so many ways. It has a good choice of selection and masking facilities, superb editing tools, sophisticated pasting and layer controls, a wealth of tonal and colour correction controls, special effect filters and powerful colour conversion capabilities.

But whilst it's undoubtedly the de facto standard for image editing, there are other capable products in the field including Live Picture and Macromedia xRes.

Fig. 2.5 Adobe Photoshop, the de facto standard for image editing

Live Picture

Although Live Picture has many features similar to Photoshop, it's essentially designed for large-scale montaging work involving elaborate image distortions. As such it's less versatile than Photoshop, being neither suitable for complex painting nor work at lower resolutions. It is heavily 'modal' and palette free. This can be off-putting to those new to the program.

The way it processes data is fundamentally different from Photoshop. Edited elements are temporarily stored as vectored objects and only rasterised once work is complete. This resolution-free method of working has the benefit of removing the time lag normally associated with editing programs.

xRes

Macromedia xRes's powerful compositing controls and paint effects tools make it ideal for large-scale montaging work. Although its interface and general controls don't match up to those in Photoshop, one can paint in near-realtime on huge files because of the way it manages its bitmapped data. Editing actions are separated from the main image data and only processed once work is complete. Although it's purely pixel based, it's unsuitable for pixel-by-pixel editing and work at low resolutions.

See also CorelDRAW! and Canvas under Draw programs.

Fonts

There are thousands of PostScript fonts to choose from for both the Macintosh and Windows systems. They are grouped into collections, some including libraries from different foundries, e.g. the Creative Alliance collection includes the Agfa, Monotype and Adobe font libraries and the Linotype collection includes the Berthold Exclusive and EF Fontinform libraries.

Size of collections
The largest collection, in terms of the number of fonts, is the Creative Alliance, with ITF coming second, the Adobe Font Folio third, Bitstream fourth and FontHaus coming in fifth place. Measuring collections on the basis of fonts can be a bit misleading as there is no fixed relationship between the number of fonts and typefaces. Typefaces can have anything from one font, as in Circle Frame MT, to nearly 60, as in Linotype's new Univers.

Classic typefaces
Whilst the size of a product range is normally no guarantee of quality, in the case of fonts, it is the case. The larger, more established, collections such as Linotype and Monotype tend to have superior designs with copyrights on most of the classic typefaces. Their products should therefore be considered before others if originals are preferred. However, Bitstream, which came late into the field, has some classic fonts of the highest quality, as they are its recent recuts of original designs.

Avant garde typefaces
It's generally the smaller foundries, such as [T-26], that produce the most mould-breaking designs. However such designs often tend to be a bit too way-out and impractical. So if you wish to employ unconventional typefaces with are less radical and consequently more usable the Take Type collection from Linotype offers an alternative source.

Kerning

Kerning – the built-in inter-character spacing of fonts – affects font quality and varies between type founderies. Agfa, Adobe and Linotype fonts are of a fairly high quality in this regard, as are Bitstream's products, although some fonts in its collection lack kerning pairs.

Font collection/library overview

- *Alias:* experimental designs.
- *Adobe Font Folio 8:* good range widely supported by bureaus. Unlocked version of Adobe's Type On Call.
- *Bitstream Typeshop and Typeshop Pro:* inexpensive range fairly well supported by bureaus.
- *Creative Alliance:* good range, including Agfa Exclusives, Monotype and Adobe collections. Widely supported by bureaus. From Monotype
- *Device:* futuristic-retro designs.
- *E Fonts:* part of the Berthold Exclusive collection.
- *Emigré:* classic avant garde designs.
- *FontFont:* modern designs.
- *FontHaus exclusives:* good non-mainstream designs.
- *ITF:* huge collection from smaller independent foundries.
- *Linotype:* high-quality designs including famous Berthold Exclusive and EF Fontinform libraries.
- *Linotype Take Type:* recent competition-winning designs.
- *MagnumType Handwriting:* impressive handwriting designs.
- *[T-26]:* mould-breaking designs.
- *Virus:* small range of modern designs.

Suppliers in UK
FontWorks: 0171 490 5390
Faces: 01276 38888

3

DTP IN USE

This chapter covers:

- **the desktop publishing process**
- **case histories showing desktop publishing in use**

Overview

In Chapter 1 I discussed how in the past design and print production involved many different disciplines, each using a variety of craft tools and technologies.

I explained how desktop publishing technology, in all its manifestations, takes over from most of these traditional methods by providing an all-embracing, multipurpose and integrated creative and production environment.

In this chapter I look at the new processes involved when working digitally by introducing you to a formal design development model.

Then, to give an idea of how desktop publishing might benefit you personally, I show you how successfully it has been adopted in different types of organisations, both large and small.

The DTP process

The overall process

The overall DTP process, like any new product development process, can be broken down into distinct phases:

1 Brief
2 Concept
3 Detail design
4 Content
5 Design production
6 Print production

Because documents vary in nature and complexity, some projects will go through all the design and production phases I cover, with each phase being completed before the next phase is started. Other projects will follow a more relaxed course, by either skipping steps or blurring the distinction between steps, e.g. layouts for simple documents can be done 'on the hoof' especially if they are more production oriented and if they don't need to embody high design values.

Also, as with any development process, there may be loopbacks in the process, e.g. changes of mind might mean that an earlier phase needs to be revisited before work can progress again.

In describing the process, I have tried to keep it as 'generic' as possible so that it is applicable to the widest range of DTP projects. (See Fig. 3.1.)

The phases

1 Brief phase

This phase involves the formulation of a design brief setting out all the project requirements and constraints. A brief would include amongst other things communication objectives, audiences, key messages, supplementary background information and technical constraints. A project budget and timescale would also be included. In the drafting of a brief, contributions may be received from many sources. Conflicting views or unreasonable ideas should be resolved before any design work commences.

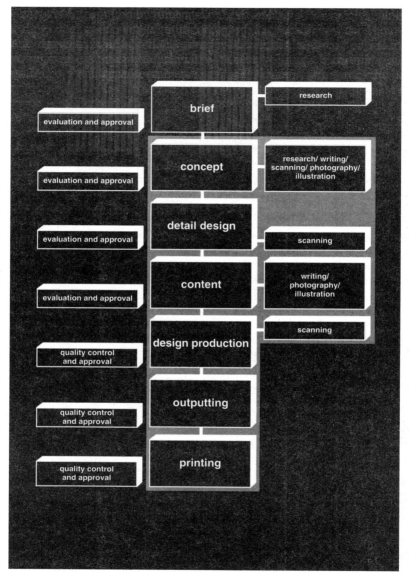

Fig. 3.1 The design and production process. Activities shown in grey panels are either partly or fully integrated into the digital process

2 Concept phase

This phase usually involves the preparation of a visual (prototype) for a document. The visual will give all those concerned with a project an idea of how the document might finally look. It will comprise page layouts in colour or monochrome of all or some of the pages. Sample text and images are included to represent the proposed editorial and visual content.

The visuals are normally printed out and bound for evaluation and assessment purposes although visuals for simple, straightforward documents may be viewed solely on-screen.

3 Detail design phase

This phase involves refining the design and/or editorial approach of the visual. Its typography, its use of images, its text; all will be reviewed and improved on as necessary. In the case of documents that will be used repeatedly templates are made. These standardised documents contain all content common to all issues of a document but no content specific to individual issues.

The document is then printed out again for further evaluation and assessment and any templates will be checked for accuracy.

4 Content phase

This phase involves the origination, acquisition and compilation of content. Text is prepared within word processors, such as Word Perfect. Optical Character Recognition (OCR) programs are sometimes employed to digitise text already typeset but not in digital form. Images are prepared by either scanning originals – photographs, illustrations and so forth – and editing them in an image processing program or by creating them from scratch within paint and draw programs. Images are also sourced from digital libraries.

All content is saved on disk in appropriate file formats.

5 Design production phase

During this phase the content is 'composed' on pages using a page layout program. Text is formatted and arranged to meet typographic needs and images positioned, cropped and scaled. As layouts progress, further content is often needed to resolve and improve layouts.

The document is then printed out for evaluation. In the case of large-scale and/or elaborate designs, proofing often takes place as work progresses.

6 Print production phase

I cover this phase in detail in the section on Printing. To summarise, print production involves pre-press activities, such as proofing, imagesetting and platemaking, and printing itself, which involves either conventional or digital presses. Throughout these processes image quality is continually monitored and controlled.

Once printing is complete, finished documents are ready for distribution.

——————— Different uses of DTP ———————

DTP is used in many areas of communication including:

- magazines, newspapers and books
- advertising and promotion
- exhibitions and point of sale
- speciality products
- information literature

The following short case histories based on real-life situations give an insight into how DTP is being used in some of these sectors and what has been gained from its employment.

Case history 1

A newspaper supplement

The Herald moved over to digital production in 1991. Whilst its broadsheet is produced on a dedicated newspaper system, its weekend supplements are produced using industry-standard programs because they offer much wider and much needed colour support.

Colour sells papers! Because QuarkXPress, Adobe Photoshop and Adobe Illustrator all handle colour well, they were chosen for the task.

There are three designer/operators and two journalists working exclusively on the supplements.

Its pages are all laid out in a series of QuarkXPress documents to enable more than one designer to work on the supplement at any one time. Most of the photographic images are scanned from colour prints on a high-end flatbed scanner and retouched and colour corrected with Photoshop. The odd image is received in digital form from picture agencies via an ISDN line.

Technical illustrations, charts, visual devices (such as logotypes) are all drawn in Illustrator. Articles are written in Microsoft Word and imported directly into QuarkXPress. Odd bits of text, such as captions and picture credits, are typed directly into the QuarkXPress documents.

The layouts of articles are done with editorial direction and the documents, once completed and thoroughly checked, are copied to a server in the pre-press department.

The pre-press operators convert the scanned images to CMYK, make any necessary tonal changes to compensate for the press performance and then send the pages via a RIP to an imagesetter for film output. The film positives are imposed by hand and then proofs are made for quality control purposes.

Desktop publishing has fulfilled all the initial requirements of management and more. Not only has it enabled colour to be easily introduced into the supplements, its adoption has given the department much greater control over the creative process. No disadvantages have been identified.

Equipment:

Computers: five Macintoshes with 21 inch colour monitors

Printers: laser printer used for medium-quality colour output from the Macintoshes

Programs: QuarkXPress for magazine layouts; Adobe Photoshop for retouching and colour correcting and montaging scans; Adobe Illustrator for technical illustrations, visual devices and charts

Scanner: Kodak multiformat transparency scanner

Imagesetter: Hyphen RIP and imagesetter

Proofers: Agfa from film-proof system

Network: Ethernet

Case history 2

Design company

Apostrophe has employed DTP technologies since the firm was founded in 1990. The design company mainly produces upmarket in-house and customer magazines for blue-chip clients. DTP enables it to offer its clients a highly streamlined and efficient service, difficult if not impossible to deliver using traditional 'analogue' means.

The bulk of its 25 staff divide roughly between copywriters and designers, with some staff concerned with sales and administration.

Design and production is concentrated in the studio, where the designers work on clients' briefs and produce visuals and where production artists produce final production files.

Their work tends to combine lively copywriting with good typography and an imaginative use of photography. The designers work almost exclusively in the digital domain; they rarely feel they need to resort to traditional media.

Their concern is to create outstanding visuals for client presentation. They are less interested in production issues and, as a result, documents are often restarted from scratch by the production artists once designs have been approved.

Is there a downside to DTP in this environment? Yes. DTP tends to restrict creativity. Techniques which are difficult to do digitally are often avoided and this leads to a degree of sameness between jobs. Furthermore DTP tends to inhibit creative thinking. The presence of a computer on their desks encourages action at the expense of reflection.

Equipment:

Computers: eight Power Macintoshes with 17 inch and above colour monitors

Printers: Apple laser printer used for low-quality colour output from the Macintoshes

Programs: QuarkXPress for magazine layouts; Adobe Photoshop for retouching and colour correcting and manipulating scans. Adobe Illustrator for creating illustrations and logotypes

Scanner: Agfa scanner

Network: Ethernet

Case history 3

Shoe company

Shoo!'s point-of-sale studio adopted DTP facilities for its design and artwork production around six years ago. Before then it used traditional artwork and reprographic methods.

All 12 of its staff were trained in the use of the Macintosh operating system and the MacroMedia FreeHand draw program; two staff were also trained in the use of QuarkXPress and Adobe Photoshop. Some staff were taught how to use an imagesetter. Digital production was phased in over a period of three months once the formal training programme came to an end.

MacroMedia FreeHand was chosen for its drawing tools, typographic features, its layer, stroke and colour controls and its general ease of use compared with other draw programs.

Trapping is of major concern when preparing artwork for silkscreen and the ability to manually set custom traps and re-layer design elements within FreeHand soon made it friends.

QuarkXPress was chosen for producing supporting leaflets and booklets and was originally considered as a host program for the FreeHand point-of-sale files. In the event, the files are output directly from FreeHand itself.

All point-of-sale artwork created within FreeHand is output on a colour printer for creative assessment. Final output to film is achieved using the studio imagesetter. Exposed films are developed in a special unit and then handed over to the silk-screen department located nearby. The silk-screen department produces wet proofs for marketing approval before proceeding with quantity production.

The adoption of DTP has enabled Shoo! to increase the efficiency of its studio and thereby reduce production costs. Amendments to artwork are much easier to make, lead times are shorter and this enables the studio to offer an enhanced design and production service to the marketing function. No disadvantages have been identified.

Equipment:
Computers: ten Power Macintoshes with 17 inch and above colour monitors
Printers: Hewlett Packard laser printer for low-quality colour output from the Macintoshes
Programs: Macromedia FreeHand for point-of-sale artwork; QuarkXPress for literature; Adobe Photoshop for retouching and colour correcting scans
Scanner: Agfa scanner
Imagesetter: Agfa imagesetter and developing unit for outputting film.
Network: Ethernet

Case history 4

Greetings card company

Xeno Cards have only recently adopted DTP facilities in-house. Like most greetings card companies it traditionally bought in all production work. The advantage of doing this was that it was able to source the best quality reprographics and printing with minimum overheads – it only needed two staff members to manage the whole of the printed output of the company. The disadvantage of sourcing everything externally was that it was incurring huge costs for client alterations. This was bad not only for the bottom line, it had the inevitable knock-on effect of discouraging any form of experimentation.

Desktop publishing promised to bring reprographic costs down to sensible levels and to give the company much greater control over the production process.

New methods of working, optimum document specifications, the most appropriate organisational setups, recruitment policies, hardware requirements, software requirements: all these aspects were thoroughly discussed before any major changes were implemented.

Xeno Cards' creative team comprises consultant art directors, staff editors, print buyers and a researcher/archivist. A middleweight DTP operator was recruited to become the first member of the new production team. He was soon joined by the researcher who manages the computerised cataloguing of images. Both were later joined by two junior operators who assist in the production of card layouts.

Desktop publishing has enabled the company to dramatically reduce reprographic costs yet at the same time give the art directors the necessary flexibility for creative experimentation. By bringing most of the production work in-house, the company has gained greater control over its workflow.

Equipment:

Computers: five Power Macintoshes with 17 inch and above colour monitors

Printers: Canon laser photocopier with Fiery RIP: used for colour photocopying flat artwork and low-quality colour output from the Macintoshes

Programs: QuarkXPress for card layouts; Adobe Photoshop for retouching and colour-correcting scans. Adobe Illustrator for creating logotypes; Canto Cumulus for cataloguing scans of card artwork

Scanner: Agfa scanner

Proofer: Imation Rainbow dye-sublimation proofer for proofing cards

Network: Ethernet

Case history 5

Railway company

When Swallow Trains took over a railway franchise in 1996, it decided to produce its timetables in-house using DTP. The previous management team produced timetables using traditional means – tables were typeset on dedicated typesetting machines, printed out on bromide, pasted onto artwork board and photographed using large reprographic cameras. The process was slow, prone to error and required long lead times.

By adopting digital methods, data could be taken directly from a central timetable database, imported into a page layout program without the need for retyping and directly output to film without recourse to camera work. Errors could be reduced to the minimum and lead times drastically shortened.

QuarkXPress was chosen for the work, partly because it was perceived as an industry standard, which gave confidence to management, partly because of its superior textbox feature and partly because of its XPress Tags function.

The idea would be for staff to cut and paste data from the central timetable database into a Microsoft Excel spreadsheet. They would then introduce special XPress Tag codes into key cells. The Excel data would then be exported as a text file and imported into specially prepared QuarkXPress templates. The tags would link with existing style sheets to automatically format the tables which would then require only the minimum of further detail formatting. Supporting text would be imported separately from normal WP files.

Seven existing PCs were upgraded with improved video cards to speed screen redraw and larger monitors were purchased so that table layouts could be viewed in their entirety at a readable size.

Staff already had Excel skills. A dedicated program of training was put in hand for the QuarkXPress training.

Adopting DTP for internal timetable production has meant a reduction in the amount of tedious copy checking, shorter lead times, lower production costs and more streamlined workflow. No disadvantages have been identified.

Equipment:

Computers: seven PCs with 17 inch and above colour monitors

Printers: laser printer for low-quality colour output from the PCs

Programs: QuarkXPress for page layout; Microsoft Excel and Word for XPress Tags work

Network: Ethernet

4

THE CREATIVE DESKTOP

This chapter covers:

- deciding on document formats
- designing layouts
- working with typefaces
- formatting type well
- creating informative diagrams
- working with images
- using colour
- organising text

Overview

This chapter is intended to give guidance on getting professional-looking results in your printed work, whatever its intended purpose or form. In each of eight areas, I explain the fundamentals and suggest areas for consideration, whether it's to do with an aspect of design or production.

Where appropriate I cover the conventions and rules which guide the professional in his or her work. For the beginner, adherence to such rules ensures a level of reader acceptability; flouting them risks being unconventional, which in itself is no bad thing. However, unless suitable alternative solutions are arrived at, deviating from accepted norms may lead to poor communication and unfulfilled objectives.

— Deciding on document formats —

There are several things one needs to consider when starting a DTP project, not least the document's page size, printing stock, method of folding and binding.

How big should the page size be? Should it be based on an ISO size or a British size? How should the document be folded and bound? Should a loose-leaf system be preferred or a fixed binding? What sort of paper and/or board stock should be used?

All these questions will need answering before any serious design work can begin, although the final choice of paper/board stock may be deferred to later in the design process.

Each project will no doubt have factors limiting formatting choice, e.g. newspaper and books are constrained by printing press sizes; press advertisements by formats offered by individual publications; mail-order items by off-the-shelf container sizes and postal cost structures. But whilst these may severely limit choice, they act as positive constraints and become part of the material consideration of a project.

In the main, document formatting tends to be design-led. Ideas generated from a brief will suggest particular solutions. Personal preference may play its part but the overriding consideration must be fitness for purpose: how well a format meets the handling, communication, filing and retrieval needs of a document.

Page sizes

Constraints on sizes

All jobs are constrained to some degree by available sheet sizes for a given paper or board stock. Paper suppliers stock only standard sizes to meet the everyday needs of commercial and specialist printers. You can of course order non-standard sizes direct from a paper mill (such orders are termed ex-mill), but the cost is usually prohibitive and delivery times invariably long.

ISO A series (trimmed)

	mm	*inches*
A0	841 × 1189	33.1 × 46.8
A1	594 × 841	23.4 × 33.1
A2	420 × 594	16.5 × 23.4
A3	297 × 420	11.7 × 16.5
A4	210 × 297	8.3 × 11.7
A5	148 × 210	5.8 × 8.3
A6	105 × 148	4.1 × 5.8
A7	74 × 105	2.9 × 4.1
A8	52 × 74	2.1 × 2.9
A9	37 × 52	1.5 × 2.1
A10	26 × 37	1 × 1.5

ISO B series (trimmed)

	mm	*inches*
B1	708 × 1000	27.9 × 39.4
B2	500 × 708	19.7 × 27.9
B3	353 × 500	13.9 × 19.7
B4	250 × 353	9.8 × 13.9

Table 4.1 ISO A and B sizes

In the UK, pages tend to be based on either the ISO A or B sizes (Table 4.1) or traditional British paper sizes (Table 4.2).

Smaller sheet sizes in either system are often supplied as trimmed (finished) sizes; most larger sizes, however, are usually available only as untrimmed sizes – they are oversize to allow space for a printing press's grippers and for printed items running to the edge of the page.

In the ISO A series untrimmed sizes are prefixed SR and R respectively, e.g. SRA2 allows for both grippers and bleed whereas RA2 allows for grippers only.

ISO paper sizes

The ISO sizes are all based on the Root 2 proportion (Fig. 4.2), the largest size A0 being 1 m^2. Subdivisions are given ascending numbers: half A0 is called A1; half A1 is A2; half A2 is A3; half A3 is A4; half A4 is A5; and so on (Fig. 4.1).

ISO sizes are also available as B sizes, which are midway in size. These intermediate sizes are useful for jobs which happen to fall

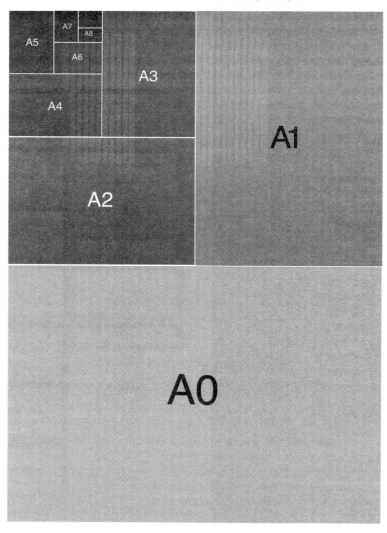

Fig. 4.1 ISO system: A sizes. How they relate to one another.
Shown at one-twelfth scale

between the A size range. However, it's worth noting that as most suppliers don't normally stock B sizes, B size documents are usually printed on sheets to the nearest A size and trimmed down, with consequential paper wastage.

Some printed items use further subdivisions of the ISO sizes. For instance, two-thirds A4 letterheads are often used as an alternative or supplement to A4 versions and one-third A4 is commonly used for compliment slips.

A8 is often chosen as a basis for business cards but because it tends to look out of proportion when printed, its length is sometimes extended by 5 mm.

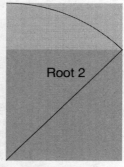

Fig. 4.2 The Root 2 proportion governs all ISO A and B sizes

The ISO sizes, particularly the A sizes, are widely used in Europe for business literature. Journals, reports and stationery items all tend to conform to this standard. Its consistent proportions give coherence to printed ranges and since most commercial printing machines are designed to the ISO series, using this system makes best use of presses and papers and boards.

Digital press paper sizes

Digital presses are either web or sheet fed. Trimmed sizes are limited by sheet widths in the case of web systems, and sheet heights and widths in the case of sheet-fed systems. (See Table 4.2)

A3 and tabloid page sizes as well as very long formats (the systems can print continuously along the paper's length) can be printed on all web systems. The printable area on sheet-fed systems allows tabloid pages to be printed in their entirety but not full A3 pages.

Digital web presses (maximum image area)

	inches
Agfa Cromapress	12 × 72
Xeikon DCP Series	12 × (other dimension subject to web length)

Digital sheet-fed presses (maximum image area)

	inches
Scitex Spontane	11 × 17
Heidelberg DI 46-4	13 × 18
Indigo E-Print	12 × 18

British (untrimmed)

	inches
Crown	15 × 20
Double crown	20 × 30
Quad crown	30 × 40
Demy	17.5 × 22.5
Small demy	15.5 × 20
Double demy	22.5 × 35
Quad demy	35 × 45
Foolscap	13.5 × 17
Small foolscap	13.25 × 16.5
Double foolscap	17 × 27
Quad foolscap	27 × 34
Imperial	22 × 30
Medium	18 × 23
Double medium	23 × 36
Post	15.25 × 19
Large post	16.5 × 21
Double large post	21 × 33
Royal	20 × 25
Double royal	25 × 40

British (trimmed)

	inches
Letter	8.5 × 11
Tabloid	11 × 17
Legal	8.5 × 14
Folio	8.5 × 13
Ledger	17 × 11

Table 4.2 Digital and British sizes

British paper sizes

The British sizes are all given names and subdivisions of the sizes are also named: the full sheet is called a broadsheet; half that is a folio, half that is a quarto, half that is an octavo, half that is a 16mo and half that a 32mo.

Folding methods

Methods of folding are always considered along with choice of paper size and binding.

The single fold is perhaps the simplest method (Fig. 4.3). This is used for many types of printed items. The gate fold (double fold), the concertina (either double or continuous fold) and parallel fold are other popular forms. Like the single fold, they are simple to produce and unless combined with other sheets don't require binding.

Fig. 4.3 The single fold, gate fold and concertina

The right-angle fold (Fig. 4.4) provides the basis for most brochure, magazine and book production. By folding a sheet several times and trimming off one set of folded edges, sets of 8, 16 or 32 pages are created. Gathering page sets together enables a large number of pages to be bound together as a single unit.

Fig. 4.4 The right-angle fold

The printed position of pages on sheets is determined by the way the sheets are folded and how they are gathered together. Invariably the order and arrangement of pages on unfolded sheets differs from the running order of a finished document so special imposition programs are employed to reorder and rearrange pages before documents are imageset.

Binding methods

The choice of binding is usually considered along with folding methods and the choice of paper. Binding methods divide into loose leaf or permanent, with some systems allowing pages to lie absolutely flat when opened.

Other factors to be taken into account when considering a binding method are unit cost and whether the binding needs to be done in-house or can be sourced from a printer or finishing house.

Looseleaf methods

Channel binding systems, including plastic grip and metal spines, are perhaps the simplest forms of binding. They slide or clamp over a square-backed or single-fold cover by means of the tension in the plastic or metal material. Pages can be added or removed fairly easily with these systems but pages cannot be opened out flat. This limits their appeal.

Fig. 4.5 Half-Canadian cover

Plastic comb and wire binding systems are superior to grip spines in that they do allow pages to open out flat. Their open rings clamp through rectangular slots punched along the inner edge of pages. Such spines are ideal for short-run documents and wire bindings are particularly elegant in appearance. Both types can be applied using fairly inexpensive and compact desktop devices and if you wish documents to have spines, covers can be half-Canadian, with front, spine and back covers printed as one sheet and bound so that the spine encloses the ring system (Fig. 4.5).

Binders with rings or posts are ideal for containing pages which need to be updated easily. Their rings or posts spring open to allow for the insertion of prepunched sheets. They allow pages to open out flat but are expensive and only suitable for very short runs.

Permanent binding methods

Saddle-stitched with wire or thread is one of the simplest and cheapest forms of permanent binding and the only one which allows pages to open flat. Wires (staples) run along the line of a single crease.

Side-stitched with wire or thread, unlike saddle-stitched, is suitable for documents with a square spine. The wires (staples) are punched through the cover and inner pages from front to back.

Section-sewn with thread is the most permanent binding method. Sections of pages are gathered side by side and sewn, first as sections and then as a complete document.

Thermoplastic (perfect binding) is a neat-looking and popular method of binding. Sections of pages are gathered, then trimmed on the back edge, which is first roughened and then impregnated with a hot plastic glue before a cover is fitted. This method is used widely in magazine and book publishing as it is inexpensive compared with the section-sewn method. If you need to bind short-run business documents in-house, compact desktop binding systems are available using a similar technology.

Setting page sizes within programs

Page sizes are set within programs in document setup controls (Fig. 4.6). Most allow you to choose from a standard range of sizes in addition to any custom size you wish to use. For most documents the page setting will match the trimmed page size. In others it will be based on the printed area only, e.g. display advertisement documents should be based on the advertisement's dimensions.

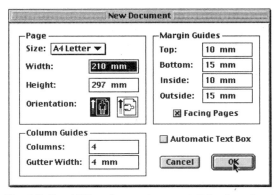

Fig. 4.6 QuarkXPress's new document dialog box showing the page size pop-up menu and fields

Facing pages or non-facing pages?

Most programs allow you to choose either facing pages or non-facing pages. If a document has a central spine and both its left and right-hand pages are being printed on, then facing pages should normally be specified. Effectively this 'mirrors' the right-hand page grid on left-hand pages.

If a document has no central spine or a central spine which is one of many, such as you would find in a concertina binding, then facing pages should not be specified.

—————— Designing layouts ——————

Defining grids

Once a document's page size and method of binding have been established, you can move on to aspects of design. But first foundations need to be put into place to provide the necessary page structures – the margin and column areas in which layouts can be developed.

The invisible intersecting lines which define such page structures are called grids and their purpose is to give rigour and order to layouts and to provide a level of design consistency between pages.

Basically you can choose between three main grid types: baseline, column and modular. The three types are often used in combination (Fig. 4.9).

Whether you choose a column or modular grid, with or without a baseline grid, will be determined as much by your design philosophy as by your document's format, subject matter, content and use.

Reference documents containing many types of information, such as encyclopedias, need complex grids to provide the necessary spatial relationships between elements whereas documents containing a single type of information presented in a linear manner, such as novels, rely only on simple grids for their success.

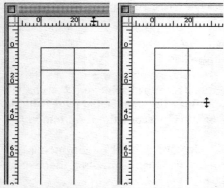

Fig. 4.7 Adding supplementary grid lines to a page

The degree to which grids impose a discipline on page layouts is as much to do with the intent of the designer as the design of the grid itself. Some designers prefer a grid to dictate the precise positioning and scale of every item, whatever its function; others are more relaxed about a grid's use.

Deciding on margin widths

All documents have constraints on the placing of type and images, not least stationery items. Constraints are imposed on such items by printing and finishing processes and the way items are intended to be read, filed and retrieved.

Margins for multipage documents are further constrained by the type of binding employed, by the design and position of headers and footers and by considerations of page yield.

Some binding methods intrude onto the page or prevent pages from opening flat. Margins need to be wide enough to allow for the encroachment of a binding system whether actual or visual. Headers, footers and page numbers are often positioned in margins and so margins need to be wide enough to accommodate them. But if margins are too wide, there is less room for text, which results in a low page yield – fewer words per page for a given font, font size and leading.

The proportion of column area to margin area is an important aspect of some documents, particularly books where often a single column of text needs to sit comfortably and elegantly within the page area.

Simple grids

Documents which have a minimum amount of text, such as letter-heads and pictorial posters, usually require only very simple grids for positioning and alignment purposes (Fig. 4.8).

Since stationery items are often bound by recipients, their left margins (their right margins on reverse sides) need to be correctly set. The positioning of key text, e.g. addressee details on letter-heads, invoices and such like need to be suitably aligned to register with envelope windows; otherwise such text may partially be hidden from view.

Column grids

Column grids simply divide the area between page margins into vertical text areas (Fig. 4.9). The more columns a grid has, the more permutations are available to a designer. Horizontal grid lines are invariably used in conjunction with such grids to create alignments between elements in adjacent columns.

Column grids are used in all sorts of publications, from the most utilitarian to the prestigious. In A4 size documents, between one and five columns is usual. In larger formats, such as broadsheets, eight to ten columns are commonplace.

In order to give yourself a large number of design permutations or to create asymmetric layouts, you can create multiple columns of a very narrow width. Body text can then span across two or more columns, with the single column used for small pictures or narrow-set captions.

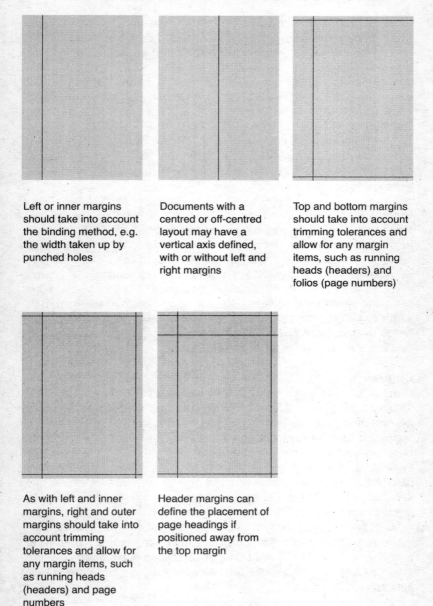

Left or inner margins should take into account the binding method, e.g. the width taken up by punched holes

Documents with a centred or off-centred layout may have a vertical axis defined, with or without left and right margins

Top and bottom margins should take into account trimming tolerances and allow for any margin items, such as running heads (headers) and folios (page numbers)

As with left and inner margins, right and outer margins should take into account trimming tolerances and allow for any margin items, such as running heads (headers) and page numbers

Header margins can define the placement of page headings if positioned away from the top margin

Fig. 4.8 Setting guides for stationery items and other simple pieces of literature

Modular grids

Modular grids divide the area within page margins into rectangular text/picture areas of suitable proportions (Fig. 4.9). A type of grid much favoured by Swiss designers in the 1960s, it gives a rational and democratic look to layouts; all areas appear to be of equal importance unlike in a column grid where upper items appear to be given prominence over lower items.

Grids of this type are often part of a planned relationship involving particular typefaces, font sizes, line lengths, type areas and unprinted space. They are usually designed with asymmetric layouts in mind, with left-aligned text and large areas given over to white space.

Grids with many modular areas offer a large number of layout permutations. Some designers in the past have designed composite modular grids where two grids are interposed one above the other to give an exhaustive range of permutations (Fig. 4.9).

Baseline grids

Baseline grids have a purely technical function. Their sole purpose is to ensure that lines of text are aligned horizontally on pages (Fig. 4.9). In so doing they automate the alignment process and ensure that type backs up (i.e. type on both sides of a page aligns) thus minimising unsightly print show-through on low-opacity papers.

Baseline grids demand the careful specification of interparagraph spacing: there's no point in aligning text to a baseline grid if the spacing between paragraphs is thrown out as a result.

Deciding on column numbers and widths

Deciding on the number of columns and their width involves taking into account proposed font and picture sizes within the parameters of the grid.

Bear in mind that the relationship of font size to column width governs the number of characters per line of setting. This affects not only the look of text, but its readability and feel.

Text with a low character count tends to look racy, readable and accessible, whilst text with a high character count tends to look more formal and perhaps more imposing, although much depends on other factors. An inappropriate character count could impart the wrong signals.

From a readability standpoint, the optimum number of characters per line of continuous text can vary considerably between types

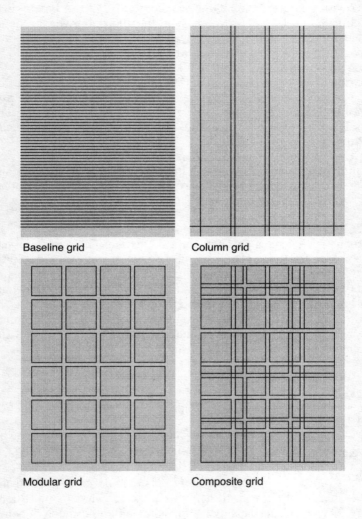

Baseline grid

Column grid

Modular grid

Composite grid

Fig. 4.9 Types of grid

of documents. For books, 60–70 would be standard. You could try a larger number of characters per line than this. With generous leading it might work; certainly anything above 90 characters per line would be too much. In news articles, between 30 and 45 characters per line is the norm.

Deciding on gutter widths

How wide gutters should be is primarily a question of design preference. Certainly the wider the gutter, the more relaxed the effect but if over-wide they significantly reduce the area for text. Narrow gutter widths (in relation to a type size) can lead to the eye reading across from column to column. To avoid this, gutters should be not less than twice the gap between the x-heights of the column text, unless a dividing rule is present.

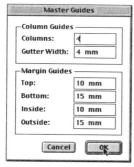

Fig. 4.10 QuarkXPress's master guides dialog box showing the column and margin guide fields

Setting page sizes within programs

Grids are usually set up within a page layout document's master pages. These pages automatically copy their content onto documents pages to which they are linked. Such content includes column and margin guides, any further additional guides and any text or pictorial content, such as page numbers.

Supplementary grid lines are usually drawn from vertical and horizontal rulers (Fig. 4.7). In some programs, such as PageMaker, sophisticated guide management controls enable complex grids to be created and edited easily by typing guide position data into fields.

Page layout pointers

There are logical sequences by which page layout designs are built up; from their beginnings as ideas in one's mind to their completion as fully formed layouts. In the previous chapter I discussed the design process. Here I give some pointers for designing documents.

Structures, relationships and running order

Ideas for layouts should only be developed once an overall structure has been devised and relationships have been established between individual pieces of content and, in the case of multipage documents, once a running order has also been established to show the linear progression of information. The process of organising the information within a document may involve rearranging content several times before everything falls into place; it's not unlike putting a jigsaw puzzle together, except there is no one single solution!

Signposting

Effective signposting – the co-ordinated use of headings, page numbers, contents tables, etc. – should be considered for documents of longer length. Since any form of signposting clarifies a document's structure it can highlight weaknesses as well as strengths in this area. For this reason signposting should be addressed early on in the design process before any detailed layout work has begun.

Layouts, grids and document formats

Whilst grid design precedes detailed page layout work, page layout ideas inform grid design, which in turn influences document formatting (Fig. 4.11). None of these aspects can therefore be considered in isolation. In each area the determining factors need to be addressed together for an optimum approach to emerge.

Treatments and idioms

Document layouts should be designed in an appropriate manner (mode of treatment) and style (idiom). For some documents, such as price lists, straightforward treatments may be all that is required whilst more complex documents, such as corporate brochures, often require treatments involving visual metaphors, pastiches and such like. Visual styles or idioms give documents their overall look and identity and whether a traditional, retro or modernist idiom is

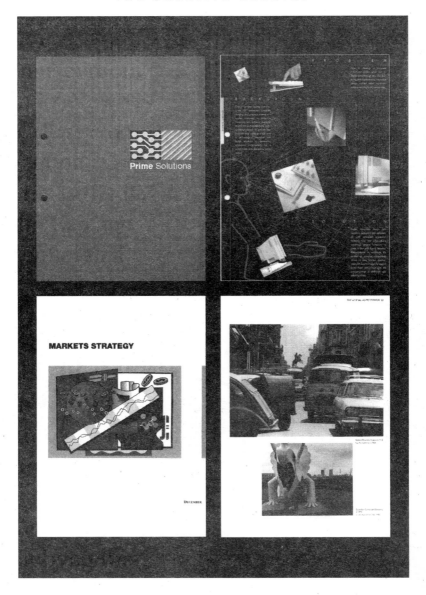

Fig. 4.11 Literature making use of grids to give structure to their layouts

appropriate depends on the main ideas governing the design approach.

Amount of text and pictures

The amount of text on document pages strongly influences their page layouts. Small amounts of text give lots of design freedom and allow white space to be used to advantage, whilst large amounts restrict the options available and preclude the use of large images. In densely packed documents, such as newletters, agreed ratios governing text and image areas usually provide the necessary editorial constraint in this area.

Aesthetic consideration of individual elements

Once all content has been allocated a place within documents, aesthetic consideration can then be given to individual elements. Should a particular image be a photograph, or treated as an illustration or diagram? Which text should be emphasised and which given a supportive role? The mode of treatment of elements depends on the main ideas governing the design approach.

Typography

Good typography is crucial to the success of layouts. The choice of typefaces, their size, leading and formatting, the position of text on the page and its relation to images: all these need to be properly addressed if page layouts are going to work from a design point of view.

Keep things simple as experienced typographers like to do since pages often look busy enough without the addition of fussy typography, and until you are expert at handling type avoid breaking typographic rules and conventions.

Formal attributes

Mass, white space, balance, contrast and symmetry should be exploited in layouts.

Layouts usually comprise text blocks, image blocks and white space. The size and massing of these components and their relationship to one another and to the page area is of prime importance.

Balance often provides the key to resolving the scale and position of such components. Unbalanced layouts usually look incomplete and may give the impression that text and images are sliding off the page. When a layout is well balanced, all components are held in equilibrium. By moving just a single component in such a layout the overall effect can easily be wrecked.

Whether a layout should be symmetrical or assymmetrical depends on many factors, not least the nature of the document in hand. Symmetrical layouts tend to be formal in feel but their axial nature can be quite restricting from a layout point of view. Assymmetric layouts on the other hand offer great scope for design and generally are more modern looking. Much of course depends on specific treatments.

Contrast enhances relationships between components and therefore gives a further dimension to layouts. For instance, a very large close-up photograph adjacent to a tiny panoramic view will give a strong sense of depth which might otherwise be lacking in a layout.

Colour

Colour should be used appropriately, i.e. to create the right mood, project a brand identity, to colour-code document sections and so forth. It should not be used for its own sake. Remember that black and white designs can look just as sophisticated as coloured ones so unless colour is supporting the communication, it's a redundant attribute. Blends and other colour effects should be used sparingly.

Experimenting

The number of layout possibilities on a page or spread is usually limitless. Good decisions may be made alongside bad. This is quite normal. The design process allows for the constant reviewing of ideas so don't be afraid to reconsider solutions or try out ideas which may at first seem unsuitable. After all, they may just work! But if they don't, amend or substitute them until you are happy with the result.

Borrowing ideas

There's no neat prescription for creating good layouts. Logic, creativity, intuition and common sense all can play their part in the process. But as a beginner you may find this all a bit too daunting. So take a leaf out of the professionals' book. Collect pieces of printed matter you consider to be well produced and relevant to the job in hand and use them as a basis for your own designs. Then follow the advice in this chapter for their detailed implementation. This way you may have a greater chance of success.

S E R I F

Sans serif

script

display

Fig. 4.12 Classes of typefaces

——— Working with typefaces ———

Typography

Type's purpose

Typography can be defined as the craft of designing with type.

Its purpose is to give 'voice' to printed items, to present the printed word in a form readable to its audience and to facilitate understanding (Fig. 4.13).

To this end, all aspects of type must be properly considered: the choice of typeface*, its size, leading, formatting, position on the page – because all these things influence the way printed matter is perceived, read and understood.

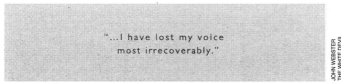

"...I have lost my voice most irrecoverably."

JOHN WEBSTER
THE WHITE DEVIL

Fig. 4.13 A setting chosen to reflect the sense of the text

Typefaces

Choosing typefaces

When choosing typefaces, begin by considering a document's audience – those who are going to read the text. Then familiarise yourself with its content, reading enough of the text to get a sense of what it's about. Next consider the type of document you are producing, whether it's a technical manual or consumer magazine, for instance.

Once you have done this you are ready to establish the right 'voice' or tone for your communication. This voice will be communicated by the typefaces you choose.

*I use the word typeface, instead of the word font which is generally used in DTP to describe individual typeface families. Strictly speaking a font is an individual character of a typeface, such as an 'a' in one weight, variant and size and not the name for the typeface itself.

Personal preference and fashion are bound to influence you but other determining factors should be a typeface's readability, the range of variants it comes in, its proportions and finally its print performance.

Classes of typefaces

The typefaces available for desktop publishing fall within five broad categories: serif, sans serif, script, display and symbol (Fig. 4.12).

Serif faces
Serif faces derive their look from the carved letter forms and scripts of Roman Italy. They have in common serifs at the end of their strokes which betray their scripted ancestry. From the Renaissance onwards there have been many classical interpretations of the serified letter forms to meet the aesthetic and technical needs of the day.

Sans serif faces
Sans serif faces date from early Victorian times. They lack serifs, the ends of their strokes being unadorned, and take their weight (boldness) from 'black letters', the gothic letters of the Middle Ages. They tend to look more streamlined than serif faces, and thus more modern looking.

Script faces
Script faces derive their form from cursive handwriting and calligraphic script. As a result their letter forms tend to join up and are generally slanting.

Display faces
Display faces were a Victorian innovation and were designed to meet the needs of commerce and advertising. Nowadays display faces come in all sorts of styles to meet practically any communication need.

Symbol faces
Symbol faces are those comprising symbols, pictograms and decorative items.

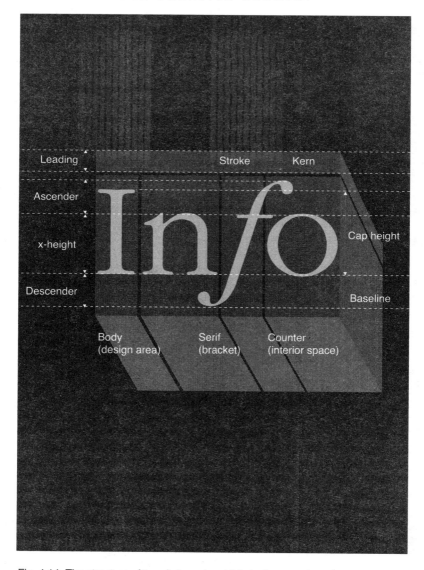

Fig. 4.14 The structure of type is based on historical convention when type was cast as three-dimensional metal fonts. The size of type is a measure of its body height, which is slightly taller than the overall printed image. The x-height for a given size varies from typeface to typeface to give longer or shorter ascenders and descenders.

Aspects of type

Readability

It is generally thought that serif settings are more readable than sans serif settings. Their serifs help to link characters into words and since we read words as units and not individual characters, theoretically this assists readability.

Furthermore, some characters in sans serif faces tend to look very alike and this makes them intrinsically less readable. For instance, the letters I and l and number 1 in some typefaces are practically identical whereas in serif faces the serifs provide the necessary differentiation.

However, much setting nowadays makes use of sans serif faces and the more we are used to reading such setting, the more readable they become and the readability gap between the two forms is perhaps closing as a result.

Certainly Roman text (often described as plain text in desktop publishing programs) is more readable than its italic version which tends to be more compressed in form.

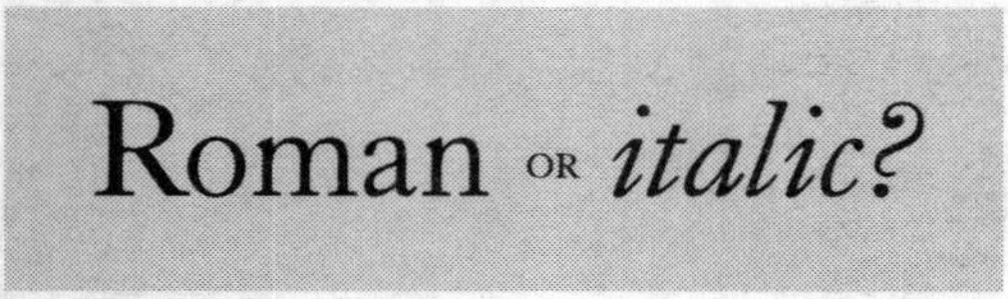

Roman OR *italic?*

Fig. 4.15

Above (Fig. 4.15) are Roman and italic letter forms in Caslon Old Face. Roman takes it name from the faces used to set the Romance languages, whilst italic takes its name from its country of origin.

Variants

Traditional serif faces tend to be restricted to one or two weights in both Roman and italic – this limits their usefulness in most contemporary work. They were designed for old style book production which did not need much typographic emphasis.

In contrast, late twentieth-century serif and sans serif designs often come in a very wide number of variants to cater for a multiplicity of contexts and uses. They are designed in families, with Roman and italic versions, each in a number of weights (light, medium, bold etc.) and sometimes in a number of widths (condensed, normal and expanded). Gill and Helvetica are examples of faces with a wide range of variants.

A modern innovation are faces which come in both serif and sans serif variants, Rotis being the first of its type.

Proportions

Typefaces differ much in overall proportion, stroke and stress (Fig. 4.14).

Some have large x-heights with short ascenders and descenders, giving them a compact look. Others have small x-heights, giving them a more open appearance. The former need not be set quite as big as the latter but invariably need to be well leaded to improve their tonal density.

Some faces are narrow, some are wide. Narrow faces give you more words per line but if too narrow they can be less readable than faces of normal width.

Letter strokes can be even in width or vary and their stress can be vertical or slanted. The strokes of serif letters usually vary and their axes often tilt backwards – as if drawn by a pen. Strokes on sans serif letters can be fairly even or quite varied in width. Humanist faces (faces inspired by Renaissance serif forms, such as Gill Sans) vary more in stroke than those based on strict geometric principles, such as Futura.

Print performance

Ever since movable type was invented by Johannes Gutenburg in the mid-fifteenth century, typeface designs have been heavily influenced by printing factors. Early designs had to be robust enough to withstand the pressure of presses yet be sufficiently fine-detailed to print legibly on rough surface papers. Each new print technology has subsequently made its impression on typeface design.

So it's not surprising that many typefaces in use today have been designed with particular printing technologies in mind. Times New Roman, for example, was designed especially for *The Times* newspaper and Century Schoolbook for general book production. Fortunately most faces work well when printed using offset-litho so a wide choice is available to you. However, if other print processes are involved it's as well to restrict your choice of faces to those suitable for the purpose in hand.

Serif and sans serif faces

Serif faces

Serif faces can be subdivided into Old Face, Transitional, Modern, Slab Serif and Twentieth-century.

Old Face designs are based on the obliquely stressed humanist script of fifteenth-century Italy. They tend to be fairly light in weight as they were originally designed for use in books. Their serifs are quite pronounced, often sloping, and their strokes are fairly even in width. They print well on antique papers but can look too thin and spidery when printed on coated papers.

Transitional faces of the eighteenth-century fall between Old Face and Modern designs and are very much influenced by the engraved work of English writers. Their stress is more vertical than Old Face designs and their serifs less bracketed. Furthermore their strokes thin out more than their predecessors. This gives them a smoother, cleaner appearance making them more suitable for printing on smooth surface stock.

Whilst Modern faces are heavily influenced by Old Face designs, early forms were very much constrained by what was achievable using engraving tools. Their stress is vertical and they have very thin cross strokes and serifs. Fat face versions have even more highly contrasting strokes, making them particularly good for display work. The sharply contrasting effects of these faces makes them eminently suitable for black and white printing.

Slab Serif faces with even-thickness strokes and block-like unbracketed serifs are termed Egyptian. They are perhaps more suitable for display work than Modern faces, often coming in a wider range of weights and proportions. Some condensed designs have serifs that are wider than their main strokes. Clarendon faces, a refined development of Egyptian, are better proportioned, and have bracketed serifs. They are more normal looking than Egyptian faces and their solid and open shapes make them excellent for printing text in newspapers.

Twentieth-century faces stem from the private press revival. Drawing more on the designer's imagination than type precedents, they nevertheless have been influenced by type features from many periods. They tend to be more Old Face in feeling than Modern if one is pressed to find a common theme amongst the designs.

Some popular serif faces:

- *Old Face:* Bembo, Ehrhardt, Galliard, Garamond, Goudy Old Style, Palatino, Plantin, Times
- *Transitional:* Caledonia, Baskerville, Bell, Fournier, Modern Extended, Modern Wide, Scotch Roman
- *Modern:* Basilia Haas, Bodoni, Melior, Walbaum
- *Slab Serif:* Calvert, Century Schoolbook, Clarion, Glypha, Ionic, Lubalin Graph, Rockwell, Serifa
- *Twentieth-century:* Joanna, Lectura, Melior, Orion, Perpetua, Pilgrim, Times

Sans serif faces

Sans serif faces can be subdivided into Geometric, Humanist, Grotesque (Grot for short) and Semi-sans.

Geometric faces are of German origin and are based on the circle and square. The resulting mechanical look certainly gives them a distinctive appearance but they can seem slightly austere.

Humanist faces combine the balance and proportion of serif faces with the simple lines of the sans serif. They have a greater warmth than most other forms of sans serif, which endears them to many typographers.

Grotesque faces are the most popular forms of sans serif. Their simple lines based on Egyptian forms appeal to the modern eye and their neutral character makes them suitable for the widest variety of texts.

Semi-sans faces straddle the serif/sans serif divide by having diminutive serifs. They tend to have an engraved feel which gives them a handcrafted quality. A recent innovation which extends this idea is faces with variants including sans serif, semi-sans and serif forms. They are useful if you wish to combine a gamut of serif/sans serif forms within involving additional typefaces.

Some popular sans serif faces:

- *Geometric:* Avant Garde, Avenir, Futura, Spartan
- *Humanist:* Frutiger, Gill Sans
- *Grotesque:* Franklin Gothic, Helvetica, Univers
- *Semi-sans/hybrid:* Albertus, Rotis

Display faces

Most display typefaces are designed to catch the eye, to convey a particular mood or a sense of style. Not surprisingly they are to be found working hard in all types of documents which require these attributes – magazines, posters, CD covers, book covers, to name but a few.

Whilst many of these faces can be difficult to read, display weights of text faces are often highly legible. These are usually given an informational role, relying very much on their legibility and neutrality for their success. They can be found in all sorts of business and public information documents where such character-istics are valued. Corporate and signage sytems (road signs, office signs, etc.) are typical applications where these types of display typeface dominate.

The gamut of display faces thus extends from the highly expres-sive and decorative to the neutral and functional. The range of faces is enormous and almost any need is catered for. However, the sheer number of faces available can be bewildering to beginners. For this reason, some designers in the past have been tempted to organise faces into personality types and to match them to specific subjects to ease the selection process.

Slab serif typefaces (faces with square serifs), for instance, would be used for documents covering industrial subjects because of their strong mechanical forms. Such a literal approach to type selection denies the designer the possible *frisson* achieved when creatively matching typefaces to subjects and should be avoided.

Script faces

Script faces provide a good foil to standard typefaces. Most are directly based on engraved or handwritten forms and as a result give a handcrafted quality to layouts. Copperplate, an obvious ex-ample of a typeface based on an engraved design, lends itself to for-mal uses. It's not surprising therefore that faces such as this are often selected for traditional-style invitations.

Other, more flowing forms based on handwriting are termed 'cur-sive' and being less formal are more useful for contemporary appli-cations.

Some faces are based on hand-drawn originals (produced with a pen, brush, pencil or other instrument). These forms are less legible than writing-based scripts and more properly belong to the display category. Mistral and Auriol are examples of such typefaces.

Symbol faces

There are symbol typefaces available for practically every subject and application, including astrology, borders and ornaments, commerce, ecology, fractions, games and sports, holidays, international symbols, logos, maths and technical, numerics, phonetics, religion, seals, television and transportation to name but a few.

The most commonly used typefaces in this category are Zapf Dingbats and Wingdings, one or both of these are supplied as standard on most systems.

Symbol or pictogram typefaces are used for a variety of reasons. Firstly they add visual interest to layouts by punctuating otherwise unarticulated text areas. Secondly they save space when substituting for regularly used words or phrases, e.g. timetables often include pictograms symbolising services to reduce space. Thirdly they provide the necessary characters for specialist and esoteric text not included in the character set of typefaces in the other main categories.

Working with faces and font sizes

Restricting the number of faces

Most professional typographers and designers tend to use a limited range of typefaces across their jobs and these are generally the classics. Some even restrict themselves to using just one type family throughout their work, but this is unusual.

Professionals restrict their use of typefaces for a number of reasons. Firstly they can get to know a few faces well and become expert at using them effectively in their work. Secondly they know that the classics perform well in most contexts and often can't be beaten. Thirdly some designers just prefer some typefaces over others and are happy to restrict themselves to these faces and ignore the rest.

This self-imposed regime may stifle typeface development but it is certainly an asset when designing. Certainly typography generally tends to look best if the number of typefaces is restricted to maybe just two or three. These could be a mix of sans serif and serif faces chosen for their compatibility or particularly for their contrast.

Restricting the number of font sizes

Restricting the number of font sizes in a document is as beneficial as restricting the number of typefaces. In the case of stationery designs, one typeface in only two weights is often sufficient.

Try to ensure that the sizes you choose are sufficiently different from one another as very small differences on a page can look unintentional.

Choosing text sizes

Font sizes for text settings are usually between 8 and 12 pt inclusive, unless text is to be read by children or those with impaired vision. In these cases, font sizes may be much larger.

The tendency is to choose larger sizes than necessary. Counteract this by choosing a size down from the one you intuitively think is appropriate and it will generally be right.

This is especially true when working on-screen as fonts can appear to be much smaller than they really are. For this reason it's always a good policy to print out samples to the proposed column width and leading to see if it looks right. Overlarge text settings tend to detract from the gravity of a subject.

Formatting type well

Aligning text

Whether text is best justified (aligned on both sides) or specified as ragged (left, centred or right aligned) depends on the nature of a document, its specific content and your intentions (Fig. 4.16).

Justified settings are economical on space, formal in appearance and work well in documents where columns are a major structural feature and information needs to be densely packed – newspapers and newletters fall into this category.

Ragged (non-justified) settings on the other hand are more informal looking and tend to work better in more open layouts, especially where white space is used to advantage.

Out of all the alignment options available to the desktop publisher, the left aligned option potentially produces the most readable settings. This is because it combines even word spacing with aligned line starts, both features contributing to reading ease. (Fig. 4.17)

Left alignment: readable, informal, rational

Centre alignment: balanced and imposing

Right alignment: a foil to the other alignments

It might be apropos to mention here that Federal finances closely resemble personal income taxes, and they add up much the same as I have demonstrated. The only difference is that in the case of Federal figures, a great many zeros can be added to the end of each item. I do not hesitate to proclaim myself one of the craftiest adders in the country (and if a president can do nothing else, he must be able to add and add). I also have an uncanny knack of describing

"Why, friends, there wasn't a lady over sixty in the whole village that I didn't raise my hat to— regularly."

WC FIELDS FIELDS FOR PRESIDENT

Responding to first-night cheers of "Author! Author!", G. B. Shaw went before the curtain only to be greeted by a lone boo. He replied, "My dear fellow, I quite agree with you, but what are we against so many?"

WC FIELDS FIELDS FOR PRESIDENT

Justified alignment: neat, fairly readable and traditional in appearance

Members originally only met on Friday nights, from October to May, for a two-hour sketching session followed by a meal and entertainment. Sketches were made to a set subject: this method of working tested the artists' retentive powers and improved their imagination.

After each sketching session was over lay members were admitted to view the results, often encouraged to purchase but definitely to partake in the meal and enjoy, and perhaps take part in, the entertainment.

In this session at the Wells Street premises, Harry Rowntree is shown in shirtsleeves and Montague Smythe is shown near right.

The dapper Montague Smythe, president in 1912, was still having pictures accepted by the Royal Academy when aged 100.

Forced justified alignment: perfect for fully justifying display text

Fig. 4.16 Examples of different alignments

Justified setting comes a close second in terms of readability as the neatness of the setting to an extent compensates for the reduction in readability caused by its uneven spacing (Fig. 4.18).

Right-aligned settings are good for relating text to pictures to their right but are difficult to read if they extend to more than a few lines in length.

Centred settings are surprisingly readable provided they are restricted to short amounts of text. They can look quite imposing because of their central axis and since both sides of the setting are non-aligned, text with extremely uneven line lengths doesn't look as ragged as it would if aligned left or right.

In display sizes punctuation at the ends of lines may upset the visual alignments. In such cases hanging punctuation should be specified so that quotation marks, for example, are positioned outside the main body of text (see example on page 5).

Don't be afraid to mix different alignments on a page. Centred headings and captions usually look good when used with justified text whatever the situation but other combinations may or may not work in particular instances.

Spacing words and characters

There is usually no need to worry about word and character spacing in unjustified text settings as they are automatically taken care of by a font's tracking and kerning tables. So unless you have copyfitting problems you shouldn't need to alter their spacing – see Tracking text in this chapter.

In justified alignments, word spacing has to vary from line to line for justification to occur but ideally it should not exceed, say, 175 per cent of the standard word spacing or the gutter width and gap between lines of text. Otherwise the reader's eye will be drawn prematurely across to an adjacent column or downwards into the next line.

Erratic and overlarge word spacing and rivers (the conjunction of unsightly spaces running downwards through areas of text) can be removed by:

- text editing
- hyphenation (breaking words locally or through the use of automatic hyphenation)
- reducing the minimum justified word spacing (in the justification control)
- negative tracking of the paragraph

Left-aligned text with even word and character spacing governed by a font's kerning and tracking tables

> This the way to the museyroom. Mind your hats goan in! Now yis are the Willingdone Museyroom. This is a Prooshious gunn. This is the ffrinch. Tip. This is the flag of the Prooshious, the Cap and Soracer. This is the bullet that...

JAMES JOYCE FINNEGANS WAKE

Justified setting with uneven word spacing and even character spacing governed by a program's justification controls

> This the way to the museyroom. Mind your hats goan in! Now yis are the Willingdone Museyroom. This is a Prooshious gunn. This is the ffrinch. Tip. This is the flag of the Prooshious the Cap and Soracer. This is the bullet that byng the...

Fig. 4.17 Word and character spacing in unjustified and justified settings

Justified display setting with fixed intercharacter spacing and local hyphenation

It is ironic that the cryptol-
ogists working entirely within
the confines of Gutenberg
technology have had no clue
or inkling of the sorts of new
environments   they   have
created.

The same setting with variable intercharacter spacing

It is ironic that the cryptol-
ogists working entirely within
the confines of Gutenberg
technology have had no clue
or inkling of the sorts of new
environments they have
created.

MARSHALL MCLUHAN AND QUENTIN FIORE WAR AND PEACE IN THE GLOBAL VILLAGE

Fig. 4.18 Justified regimes compared

Character spacing in body text shouldn't vary at all as it not only looks awful – words are stretched out by different amounts from line to line – but its employment severely reduces readability. In display settings however character spacing is often necessary to avoid large gaps between words.

Not everybody follows this rule. Because justification settings achieved by word spacing alone can easily lead to over-wide spacing in narrow columns, even when automatic hyphenation is in operation, newspapers tend not to follow it.

They invariably have neither the time nor the will to resolve the editing problems which inevitably arise from such a regime. More's the pity as uneven letter spacing in unjustified text always looks poor whatever the context.

Hyphenating text

Words tend to be broken in text settings for one of two reasons: firstly to reduce the incidence of large word spacing in justified setting and secondly to reduce the raggedness of unjustified setting.

Hyphenation in justified setting is usually essential if fairly even word spacing is to be achieved. Its use, however, should be well controlled as too many word breaks and hyphens can spoil the look of a setting.

Word breaks and hyphens in unjustified text tend to look obtrusive, whatever their frequency. This is especially so in left alignments as they occur on their ragged right-hand edge. Since unjustified alignments look best if there is a reasonable variation in line lengths and hyphenation reduces such variation, its use should generally be restricted. Hyphens work best, if at all, in unjustified work of medium line length. Short captions, and text composed of very short lines and maybe including many names, should be left unhyphenated.

Automatic hyphenation

Automatic hyphenation is usually controlled within paragraph or hyphenation dialog boxes in programs and refers to a special hyphenation dictionary for their operation.

You should set the controls to avoid two successive hyphens at the ends of lines and to avoid a hyphen in a column's last line (the latter may not be controllable automatically).

Setting showing effect of increasing leading. Notice how the letter and word spacing (tracking) look progressively tighter as the leading is increased.
Font size/leading: 8/8–21 pt

But you love her for her hessians and sickly black stockies,... isn't it the cat's tonsils! Simply killing, how she tidies her hair! I call her sosy because she's sosiety for me and she says sossy while I say sassy and she says will you have some more scorns while I say won't you take a few more schools... But you love her for her hessians and sickly black stockies,... isn't it the cat's tonsils! Simply killing, how she tidies her hair! I call her sosy because she's sosiety for me and she says sossy while I say sassy and she says will you have some more scorns while I say won't you take a few more schools... But you love her for her hessians and sickly black stockies,... isn't it the cat's tonsils! Simply killing, how she tidies her hair! I call her sosy because she's sosiety for me and she says sossy while I say sassy and she says will you have some more scorns while I say won't you take a few more schools... But you love her for her hessians and sickly black stockies,... isn't it the cat's tonsils! Simply killing, how she tidies her hair! I call her sosy because she's sosiety for me and she says sossy while I say sassy and she says will you have some more scorns while I say won't you take a few

JAMES JOYCE FINNEGANS WAKE

Mixed font sizes don't affect fixed leading. Font size/leading: 10,14/14 pt

With a floating cast of characters presided over by the charismatic Roberto the engineering department has done pioneering work in the field of industrial design and development

The effect of mixed font sizes on auto leading. Font size/leading: 10,14/auto

With a floating cast of characters presided over by the charismatic Roberto the engineering department has done pioneering work in the field of industrial design and development

Fig. 4.19 Leading settings

Leading text

Line spacing is governed by leading (pronounced 'ledding'), a term derived from the strips of lead used to separate lines of metal type in the past.

Almost all text is made more readable by the addition of leading. It 'opens up' settings, making them more accessible and in so doing alters its texture (its colour). Its judicious use is therefore essential to the attainment of good typography.

Fig. 4.20 Leading control (at top left of palette) in QuarkXPress

Care therefore needs to be taken to set the most appropriate leading values for given font sizes and column widths for colour consistency across settings (Fig. 4.20). As a general rule, the more characters per line the greater should be the leading; otherwise the setting will look progressively tighter (Fig. 4.19). Settings using typefaces with short ascenders and descenders need relatively more leading than those with smaller x-heights.

Very short lines of text may have minimal leading values, equal to or slightly *greater* than the font size (large headings may also have minimal leading values, equal to or slightly *less* than the font size). Lines of eight to ten words in length should have leading which roughly corresponds to 110 per cent of the font size. Longer lines, of course, require proportionately more leading.

If text doesn't fit at the design stage because of the addition of leading, it's best to reduce both font size and leading on a proportional basis – not just the leading alone – to maintain its colour and its readability. This technique should normally not be use for copy-fitting purposes.

Leading is normally expressed as the sum of the space and accompanying font size – it describes the repeat distance of lines of text, not the intervening space.

It can also be specified as an amount more or less than the font size, such as +2 pt or –1, or as a percentage of the font size.

This last method, usually governed by the auto setting in programs, should be avoided unless you wish on a line by line basis, for leading values to be dictated by the largest font (or anchored text box) or if you are setting leading for a single line of text, in which case leading settings are normally not applied (Fig. 4.19).

Tracking: 0; Font size/leading: 9/11.5 pt

Font size/leading: 5/7 pt

It was the best of times, it was the worst of times, it was the age of wisdom, it was the age of foolishness, it was the epoch of belief, it was the epoch of incredulity, it was the season of Light, it was the season of Darkness, it was the spring of hope, it was the winter of

It was the best of times, it was the worst of times, it was the age of wisdom, it was the age of foolishness, it was the epoch of belief, it was the epoch of incredulity, it was the season of Light, it was the season of Darkness, it was the spring of hope, it was the winter of despair, we had everything before us, we had nothing before us, we were all

Tracking: .003 en

It was the best of times, it was the worst of times, it was the age of wisdom, it was the age of foolishness, it was the epoch of belief, it was the epoch of incredulity, it was the season of Light, it was the season of Darkness, it was the spring of hope, it was

It was the best of times, it was the worst of times, it was the age of wisdom, it was the age of foolishness, it was the epoch of belief, it was the epoch of incredulity, it was the season of Light, it was the season of Darkness, it was the spring of hope, it was the winter of despair, we had everything before us, we had nothing before us, we were all

Tracking: .006 en

It was the best of times, it was the worst of times, it was the age of wisdom, it was the age of foolishness, it was the epoch of belief, it was the epoch of incredulity, it was the season of Light, it was the season of Darkness, it was the spring of hope, it

It was the best of times, it was the worst of times, it was the age of wisdom, it was the age of foolishness, it was the epoch of belief, it was the epoch of incredulity, it was the season of Light, it was the season of Darkness, it was the spring of hope, it was the winter of despair, we had everything before us, we had nothing before us, we were

Tracking: .009 en

It was the best of times, it was the worst of times, it was the age of wisdom, it was the age of foolishness, it was the epoch of belief, it was the epoch of incredulity, it was the season of Light, it was the season of Darkness, it was the spring of hope, it

It was the best of times, it was the worst of times, it was the age of wisdom, it was the age of foolishness, it was the epoch of belief, it was the epoch of incredulity, it was the season of Light, it was the season of Darkness, it was the spring of hope, it was the winter of despair, we had everything before us, we had nothing

DICKENS A TALE OF TWO CITIES

Fig. 4.21 Tracking settings compared. Text becomes progressively more open and legible the greater the tracking

Tracking text

Tracking, or range kerning as it is sometimes called, governs the character and word spacing of text. It's used to improve the legibility and readability of text, to shorten copy lengths and to change the pace of text, amongst other things.

Tracking alters the colour of text and should therefore be considered along with leading settings (Fig. 4.21).

Standard tracking (zero units of track) is normally adhered to for most text setting. This is how the font designer intended the text to be spaced so any deviation from zero should not be taken without due consideration (Fig 4.22).

However, circumstances may demand some closing up (negative tracking) or widening (positive tracking).

Settings in very small sizes (around 5 pt) and reversed-out settings usually benefit from being slightly wider spaced to improve their legibility. Very long lines may also benefit from slight additional tracking to complement high leading values.

Fig. 4.22 Kerning control in FreeHand

Increased tracking lengthens text and can improve readability. Reduced tracking shortens text and can remove widows (the short lines at ends of paragraphs) thus reducing the number of lines in a column. Tracking should not exceed –4 for this work; otherwise the adjustment will be clearly noticeable.

Display settings of, say, 18 pt and above can benefit from negative tracking, otherwise the setting may look too 'gappy'. Unless tracking is intended to letterspace selected words, it should not be varied within a paragraph.

Setting in single font size using simple paragraph spaces

11
White Arc I 1972 (CL 480)
Oil on Canvas
245×245
Stedelijk Museum, Amsterdam

12
White Arc II 1974 (CL 482)
Painted aluminium
162×513×1
Leo Castelli Gallery,
New York

19
Arc IIII 1974 (CL 485)
Steel
210.5×435.5×2
Joan & Robert Weissman
Los Angeles, California

20
Arc IX 1975 (CL 489)
Steel
350×50.5×2

25
Arc XII 1977 (CL 497)
Steel
350×25.5×2

26
Arc XIII 1978 (CL 504)
Oil on canvas
230.5×245.5
Blumfield Gallery
London

Setting in multiple font sizes locked to a baseline grid

Specialist Tours

Bicycle Tours
(Bookings: 0171 928 6838).
London Bicycle Tour Company offers two
Sunday tours: Greenwich Market excursion
(morning) and East End Tour (afternoon).
Departure 10am & 2.30pm Sun (approx 3 hour
tour). Meeting point 56 Upper Ground, SE1.
Fee £9.95. Independent bike hire from £6.95 per
day.

Docklands Tours
(Bookings: 0171 512 1111).
London Docklands Development Corporation
offer two hour coach tours with expert guides.
Departures 2pm Tues, 10.30am Thurs. Meeting
point Docklands Visitor Centre, 3 Limeharbour,
Isle of Dogs, E14 (Crossharbour DLR). Fares
£6; £5 OAPs, students, children.

Garden Day Tours
(Bookings: 0171 431 2758).
One-day trips to English Gardens and beautiful
houses, usually visiting three different gardens
per trip. Departure 8.30am Weds & Thurs
(return 6pm). Meeting point Embankment
underground (river side exit). Fares £44 per day

National Theatre Tours
(Bookings: 0171 633 0880).
Fascinating backstage tours of the National
Theatre at the South Bank (see p 97 for detailed
information). Advance booking essential.
Departures 10.15am, 12.15pm & 5.30pm
Mon–Sat. Fee £3.50; £2.50 OAPs, students,
children.

Star Safari
(Bookings: 0932 854721).
Half-day coach tours focusing on royalty, the

Setting in single font size using vertical alignment

*As part of the council's Social Services
Department, we manage and support the
Department's main Information Systems. IT is
continuing to become critical to the operations of
the Department and we are currently in the
process of expanding our wider area network to
bring the rest of the Department on-line to our
databases (Oracle 7/Lotus Domino).*

*We are looking for enthusiastic, motivated
individuals to join our lively Information
Solutions Team. You will be working in a fast
changing and often pressurised environment.
You must have good interpersonal skills, be
resilient under pressure and work well with
other members of the team.*

Fig. 4.23 Column alignments compared

Spacing hierarchy

I've discussed character and word spacing in justified paragraphs and tracking in text but how do they all work together?

Each font has its own built-in tracking and kerning tables. When you select a font, it's character and word spacing are governed by these tables.

All other spacing uses this spacing as a starting point. In justified text, the minimum, optimum and maximum percentages are based on these settings. In all alignments, any tracking and kerning at a local level is applied over and above the other regimes.

Aligning text to text

Settings which involve paragraph spaces can result in columns of uneven length and lines of type not aligning across the page.

There are a number of ways to ensure that either one or both aspects are addressed:

- by applying vertical alignment
- by using 'simple' paragraph spaces
- by using 'complex' paragraph spaces
- by using a baseline grid

Applying vertical alignment

For text settings in newsletters and other news-related documents, it may be acceptable to align the tops and bottoms of columns, leaving intervening lines to fall at will. This technique involves 'vertically justifying' lines in a column (Fig. 4.24) and since it alters paragraph and line spacing, its effect can be quite unsatisfactory unless sufficient text is in a column in the first place (Fig. 4.23).

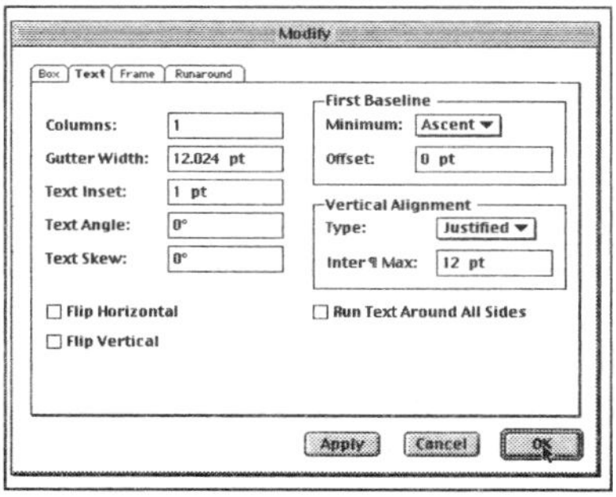

Fig. 4.24 Vertically justified control in QuarkXPress

Using 'simple' paragraph spaces

An alternative approach is to restrict the spaces between paragraphs to line spaces (spaces matching the leading value) and/or simple fractions of the leading, such as half-line spaces (spaces half the leading value).

This way, provided column tops are level and text leading is consistent lines of setting will align with adjacent settings, or if half-line spaces are used lines of setting within alternate paragraphs will align (Fig. 4.23).

Example 1

(Main text	leading	12 pt)
Space before subhead		6 pt
Subhead	**leading**	**12 pt**
Space after subhead		6 pt
Total spaces and leading		*24 pt (multiple of 12 pt)*
(Main text again	leading	12 pt)

Example 2

(Main text	leading	12 pt)
Space before		12 pt
Subhead	**leading**	**12 pt**
Total spaces and leading		*24 pt (multiple of 12 pt)*
(Main text again	leading	12 pt)

This approach inevitably limits the spacing options available to you and may not in itself align bottoms of columns. It's more suitable for text settings where the type size is constant and/or where columns heights are intended to vary.

On the positive side, the approach is easy to implement and results in a visual simplicity.

Using 'complex' paragraph spaces

An approach which offers a greater number of spacing permutations than that previously described but is much more complex to work out involves the setting of spaces which, in conjunction with other spaces, add up to multiples of the text leading.

The key to understanding how this works is to ignore font sizes altogether and concentrate on leading values. This is because font sizes in themselves don't determine line spacing (unless auto leading is in operation, in which case this approach can't be used).

The mathematics involves adding together leading values. For every intermediary paragraph involved, such as subhead paragraphs, take each leading value and multiply it by the number of lines in the paragraph. Then add any spaces before and after the paragraphs. The idea is to set leading amounts and paragraph spaces which add up to multiples of the main text leading.

Example 1

(Main text	leading	12 pt)
Space before		6 pt
First line subhead	**leading**	**14 pt**
Second line subhead	**leading**	**14 pt**
Space after		2 pt
Total spaces and leading		*36 pt (multiple of 12 pt)*
(Main text again	leading	12 pt)

Example 2

(Main text	leading	11 pt)
Space before subhead para		6 pt
Single line subhead	**leading**	**12 pt**
Space after subhead para		4 pt
Total spaces and leading		*22 pt (multiple of 11 pt)*
(Main text again	leading	11 pt)

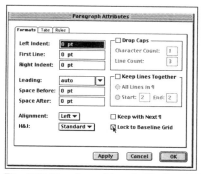

Fig. 4.25 Baseline grid control in QuarkXPress

Using a baseline grid

A final approach is to align the baseline of body text to an invisible page grid (Fig. 4.25). This way, lines are forced into alignment whatever the paragraph spaces employed. Were it that simple! Having the baseline grid override spaces is quite unsatisfactory so it's an approach which really needs to be used in conjunction with the one just outlined (Fig. 4.23).

Combining the approaches

The different alignment approaches can be combined in a number of ways to meet specific needs.

Here are some possible combinations:

- vertical alignment alone
- 'simple' paragraph spaces alone
- 'simple' paragraph spaces with baseline grid
- 'complex' paragraph spaces alone
- 'complex' paragraph spaces with baseline grid
- 'complex' paragraph spaces with vertical alignment
- baseline grid alone

Preventing orphans from upsetting column alignment

Orphans are the last lines of paragraphs positioned by chance at tops of columns. As they are often short in length they prevent columns from looking optically aligned along their top edges.

Orphans can be automatically eliminated by keeping the first and last two lines of paragraphs together. So instead of a short line appearing at the top of a column, the line preceding the potential orphan also moves up to the top, thereby providing a first full line of text.

However, an extra line needs to be created to fill the depth of the preceding column; in the case of single-column books it's common practice to leave columns one line short in these situations.

In most page layout programs orphans are automatically controlled as part of paragraph formatting by checking 'Keep (lines) together' and entering 2 in the start and end fields (Fig. 4.26).

Removing unsightly widows

The discussion of orphans leads on to widows, the short lines at the ends of any paragraphs. These should be removed if they look too unsightly. Their removal will reduce the numbers of lines, which may or may not be of benefit to you from a copyfitting point of view.

Widows are removed by text editing, negative tracking, hyphenation or in justified setting reducing the minimum word spacing in the paragraph control from, say, 85 to 75 per cent or less.

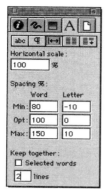

Fig. 4.28 'Keep (lines) together' widow control in FreeHand

Defining paragraphs

Paragraphs conventionally begin on a new line. Their starts can be emphasised by indenting their first lines and/or by introducing spaces before them. Either way, readers do not have to rely solely on the presence of a short line at the end of preceding paragraphs to indicate paragraph breaks.

Indents can be used in both justified and ragged settings and their width is usually based on the setting's font size, e.g. if the font size is 10 pt then the indent can be 10 pt, 15 pt, 20 pt etc. The longer the indent the more relaxed the effect. Indents less than the font size invariably look too mean and should generally be avoided.

Paragraph spaces used by themselves look good, but since they are space consuming they tend to be more appropriate for layouts where white space is used to advantage.

For section starts, drop capitals or the setting of the first few words in small capitals can provide suitable emphasis.

Hanging indents may occasionally be appropriate in text, although their use is normally restricted to listed items. Bullet points or numbers can 'hang' within the empty spaces created by the indents, provided they are wide enough to accommodate them. Hanging indents can be progressively adjusted from paragraph to paragraph to created a nested look. (See Fig. 4.27 and Fig. 4.28.)

The limitation of hanging indents – that only one line can extend out to the left of the main body of a paragraph – can be overcome by

Nested hanging indents

Drop cap as design feature

Sanity clauses

Negative first line indent

← **I.** When a you

Positive left indent

→ prospective

Negative first line indent

← *a)* Never

Positive left indent

→ show u

b) Do no

employ

questic

c) Remen

liquor

person

d) Offer y

prospe

pull.

e) Never

mind.

eturning to the system of deposits would give people an incentive to take action, Christopher believes. It would get us

Hanging indents

Let's make a resolution true,
    And firm and good and healthful, too,
But we must promise when we make it,
    That we shall never, never—

WC FIELDS FIELDS FOR PRESIDENT

Character-based indents staggering text

They reel

to and fro, and

s t a g g e r

like drunken

men:

and are at

their wit's end.

BOOK OF COMMON PRAYER

Fig. 4.27 Paragraph formatting examples

the use of anchored (sometimes termed in-line) text areas. Within these boxes any number of lines can be set and to any alignment.

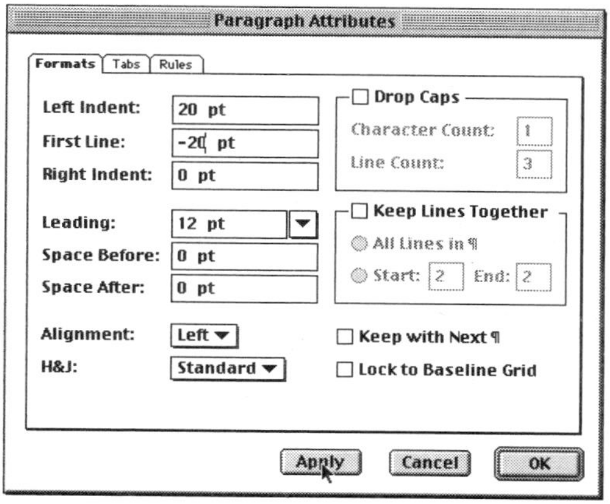

Fig. 4.28 Hanging indent setting in QuarkXPress

Staggered indents (indents which alter their position on a line-by-line basis) can be useful in specialist copy where text needs to align with specific words for clarity. Such indents are often character based, being entered using 'Indent here' commands.

Tabulating text

Types of table structure
Tables are approached in a number of ways within DTP programs. Usually they are paragraph based: text is typed from left to right as for normal setting and separated, as required, into paragraphs. Column alignments are then specified within each paragraph, along with other attributes, such as spacing and rules. Alignment options usually include left, right, centred and decimal. Some programs even include a 'Based on' alignment to vertically align text to a user-specified character, such as an 'x' (Fig. 4.30).

Tables in some programs are cell based: text is typed into separate cells, as in a spreadsheet. Cell-based systems not only allow text to flow vertically within cells, they allow you to alter the height and width of cells, to add tints and borders and to apply colour attributes.

Single block of text composed of tabbed paragraphs separated by horizontal rules

Performance feature	System telephone T611-0	Cordless System telephone SCT 611-0¶
Hands-free	• separate button	¶
Dialling without lifting the receiver	• separate button	¶
Speakerphone function	• separate button	¶
Display	2-line text	16-digit¶
Light button	•	•¶
Door release button	•	•¶
Charge metering/display	•	¶
Call duration display	•	•¶
Dial repeat	Extended dial repeat (notebook)	up to 3 call numbers ¶

Separate blocks of framed and panelled text snapped to a baseline grid

Technical information

substance g/m²	200	225	250	275	300	350
gloss (Gardner) 75°	75	75	75	75	75	75
caliper µm (approx)	155	185	200	230	260	300
opacity (EEL)%	–	–	–	–	–	–
rigidity (Taber) 15° MD	1.8	2.6	3.7	4.7	5.9	10.0
mN m CD	1.1	1.7	2.4	2.6	3.4	5.5
surface pH	7.1	7.1	7.1	7.1	7.1	7.1

Fig. 4.29 Table methods compared

Rules and colours

There is usually no need to add vertical rules or to box paragraph-based tables as their columns stand out without the need for such devices. Good use of horizontal rules, however, can improve appearance and aid clarity. Cell-based tables, being inherently 'boxy', look good tinted, with or without rules and borders. (See Fig. 4.29.)

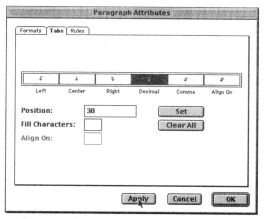

Fig. 4.30 Tabulation control in QuarkXPress

One problem with cell-based tables is that if you need subsequently to convert the text into a paragraph-based table, a great deal of editing is required to get the text in the right order.

Lining figures – numbers with the same body width – should be used for tabular work, especially for financial subjects, as their figures align vertically within columns. Most modern typefaces have lining figures but it's worth checking to see if the font you propose to use for a table is correct in this regard.

Tabular forms

One can consider forms – application forms, tax forms and such like – as being complex tables. Many of these types of forms can be constructed out of either paragraph-based or cell-based tables or a combination of both. Obviously any form design needs to take into account the constraints of the table constructions employed.

Some forms may be best composed out of standard page layout components, in the case of QuarkXPress out of text and picture boxes. Used in conjunction with a baseline grid and ruler guides, the boxes can be accurately scaled and positioned to meet the most demanding positional constraints.

However, one problem arises when you frame abutting boxes. Because frames in some programs don't straddle box sides you get a double-width effect when boxes are abutting. The way to solve this problem is to overlap boxes by the same amount as the frame width. By doing this frames will print directly on top of each other.

Emphasising words within text

Selected words within text can be emphasised in a number of ways: by using typestyles or variants of the same font such as italic or bold, by using entirely different fonts or by using colour or tone.

Italics are perfect for giving stress to a sentence. Their use can also remove the need for punctuation, e.g. publication names can be set in italics rather than within quotation marks.

CAPITALS give strong emphasis but they can stand out too much in certain situations. In such cases, reduce their size fractionally and slightly track the characters.

SMALL CAPS are a good alternative to caps as their letters are in scale with the lower-case letters they accompany but they have an old-fashioned appearance which precludes their use in most contemporary documents.

Bold settings give strong emphasis but can sometimes make the text look too spotty.

Light settings oddly enough can also give emphasis but sometimes the negative effect can make the text look a bit weak.

Underlining, a hangover from the days of mechanical typewriting, invariably looks crude and should generally be avoided.

Different fonts can emphasise words in interesting ways, but care needs to be taken to ensure that they work well together, especially if their x-heights differ too much.

You can of course use different font sizes to emphasise text, in conjunction with other methods or not. This can present difficulties within settings if leading values are to be maintained unless you restrict its use to first lines of paragraphs.

Whichever methods are used, care needs to be taken in styling accompanying punctuation. Commas and full stops, for instance, should only be emphasised along with text if it makes sense to do so.

Key Cap	Char.	Shift-char.	Alt-char.	Alt-Shift-char.	Key Cap	Char.	Shift-char.	Alt-char.	Alt-Shift-char.
A	a	A	å	Å	Y	y	Y	¥	Á
B	b	B	∫	ı	Z	z	Z	Ω	Û
C	c	C	ç	Ç	1	1	!	¡	/
D	d	D	∂	Î	2	2	@	™	◻
E	e	E	x	‰	3	3	£	#	‹
F	f	F	ƒ	Ï	4	4	$	¢	›
G	g	G	©	Ì	5	5	%	∞	fi
H	h	H	·	Ó	6	6	^	§	fl
I	i	I	^	È	7	7	&	¶	‡
J	j	J	Δ	Ô	8	8	*	•	°
K	k	K	°		9	9	(	ª	·
L	l	L	¬	Ò	0	0	)	º	‚
M	m	M	µ	˜	`	`	~	`	Ÿ
N	n	N	~	ˆ	-	-	x	–	—
O	o	O	ø	Ø	=	=	x	≠	±
P	p	P	π	Π	[	]	x	‘	’
Q	q	Q	œ	Œ	]	[	x	“	”
R	r	R	®	Â	\	\	x	«	»
S	s	S	ß	Í	;	;	x	…	Ú
T	t	T	†	Ê	'	'	x	æ	Æ
U	u	U	¨	Ë	,	,	x	≥	¯
V	v	V	√	◊	.	.	x	≥	˘
W	w	W	Σ	„	/	/	x	÷	¿
X	x	X	≈	Ù	space bar				

Fig. 4.31 Standard character set on the Apple Macintosh

Styling characters

Standard character sets

The standard character set for fonts includes the letters of the alphabet in upper and lower case, small caps, accented characters and ligatures, figures, punctuation marks, some fractions and selected devices, such as copyright marks.

Most of these characters are accessible via the keyboard (Fig. 4.33). Some can only be accessed by special keystrokes or by entering an ANSI or ASCII code number.

Some extended fonts include non-aligning numerals. Sometimes called old-style or lower-case figures, these numerals ascend and descend from the x-height of the font in the same way as characters such as 'h' and 'p'. They are designed to integrate well with lower-case characters but their old-fashioned appearance precludes their use in most documents.

Kerning characters

Whilst tracking governs the overall spacing of characters, kerning governs the spacing between individual characters. Each font has its own built-in kerning tables, comprising kerning pairs. When you select a font its intercharacter spacing is governed by these tables.

The set kerning can be altered at a local level (Fig. 4.32) to correct unsatisfactory spacing within displays or to create interesting typographic effects, e.g. the design of logotypes inevitably involves precise kerning work along with other typographic manipulation.

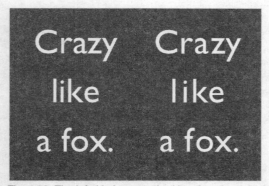

Fig. 4.32 The left title has standard kerning; the right title has been respaced and centred

Local kerning is usually restricted to large settings as it's impracticable to kern text at smaller sizes because of the amount of work usually involved. In any case poor intercharacter spacing is generally less disturbing to the eye at small font sizes. However, there are exceptions. Character pairs, such as fl, consistently look too widely spaced without special kerning (compare fl with fl, the former looking too widely spaced, the latter looking just right). Fortunately such pairs are usually supplied as ligatures – joined characters – obviating the need for repetitive local kerning work (Fig. 4.33).

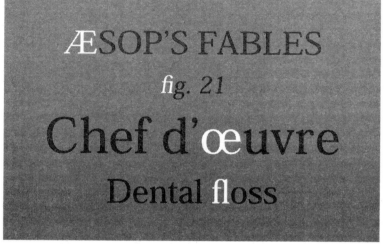

Fig. 4.33 Ligatures in the ASCII set highlighted

Most standard fonts only have one or two ligatures for tight fitting, the rest are supplied for European language setting. Happily, typefaces with 'extended' fonts are available with a wider range of ligatures should they be deemed to be necessary.

Footnotes and fractions

Characters can be raised or lowered using the Superscript and Subscript typestyles, and raised and reduced in size for footnote figures using Superior[1]. Characters can also be moved up or down relative to the baseline using a Baseline-Shift control. This control is particularly useful if you wish to alter the vertical position of type without altering leading values.

Some standard character sets include simple fractions – most don't. Special fraction fonts are available but the range of typefaces they come in is severely limited. If you are not able to justify purchasing a special fraction font or a suitable font is not available in the typeface you require, fractions can be 'jury-rigged' using standard numerals. By raising, lowering and reducing the size of numerals either side of an oblique stroke, fractions can be made in a typeface of your choice, e.g. $^{124}/_{345}$.

———— Working with images ————

The role of images

Images, whether photographic or illustrative, have always been a powerful adjunct to the printed word. Unlike type they deliver their message immediately, often conveying information which words could never adequately describe, however many one used.

It's not that images are superior to words. It's just that words and images are a natural pairing. Together they communicate more effectively than either form can do by itself.

The important thing to recognise is that images, by attracting the eye, draw us into a page. Together with captions and display text they invite us to peruse and then read a document. If they are pertinent and well crafted they reinforce communication by favourably manipulating the viewer's perception of a document and its subject matter.

Are photographs more effective than illustrations in doing all this? And when should one form be preferred over the other?

Since the camera is better at recording the outward appearance of things, photography must be the preferred medium when likeness matters. However, illustrations can elucidate and reveal in ways which photographs can't. They can be in many forms – drawing, painting, scribbles – but always the question of style arises. This is both their strength and their weakness. The graphic style of an illustration gives it its individuality yet this very individuality inevitably reduces it universal appeal.

Whatever choices you make, images need to be soundly crafted to reproduce well on the page. So in this section I not only cover sources for photographs and illustrations but discuss those technical aspects which affect image quality.

Using off-the-shelf images

You may decide to draw or photograph images yourself or commission or buy images from external sources, such as photographers and photo libraries.

If you have the right skills, sufficient time or the inclination to originate content yourself, this route can be the most satisfying to take. But even if you prefer to do everything yourself, some subjects will be totally inaccessible to you, such as subjects of a historical nature or images from outer space – in which case you will have no choice but to source such images from image libraries (Table 4.3).

Some collections or libraries are in the public domain (they are free to anyone who wishes to use them); others are available from commercial organisations (Fig. 4.34) or are given away when you purchase graphics programs .

Some libraries, such as PhotoDisc, comprise specially commissioned images; others, like Hulton Getty and Corbis, are akin to traditional picture library collections.

The former tend to give you unlimited licence to use and alter their work; the latter copyright their work, which means individual images can only be reproduced after payment of a fee.

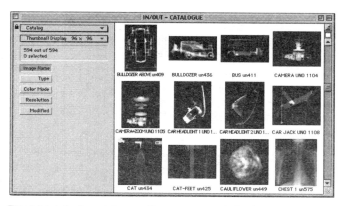

Fig. 4.34 In/out's catalogue of images presented using Canto Cumulus, a visual cataloguing program

Off-the-shelf images vary enormously in quality from the truly awful to the exceptional. Images are either vectored or bitmapped; the former are scalable to any size without any reduction in image quality.

Image collections can usually be browsed on CD-ROMs which include low-resolution files suitable for composing design visuals and high-resolution images in the case of royalty free images.

You can work in one of two ways with some royalty free libraries. You can specify a subject area or theme and, for a fee, the library will provide a disk comprising the specially collected images. Alternatively you can choose from a standard range of themes or subject areas.

Using digital cameras

Whilst taking photographs with digital cameras is not much different from conventional photography, there are certain things which need to be taken into consideration.

Though digital cameras share some technology with conventional cameras – such as lenses and iris diaphragms – their different imaging method requires a modification of approach.

Firstly their viewing is often smaller than on equivalent conventional cameras as their CCD sensors tend to occupy a smaller area than a frame of film. This gives a smaller viewing angle and thus the effect of a longer focal length.

Secondly though CCD sensors have a fixed response to light – as does film – there's no need to use filters to compensate for types of light sources as white balance can be adjusted within their controls. Choosing a tungsten setting, for instance, will either increase the time allowed for the blue and green charges to build up or will amplify the blue and green signals after capture. One or other of these methods is also used to compensate automatically for the fact that CCD sensors are more sensitive to the red end of the spectrum.

Thirdly whilst digital cameras are theoretically able to capture a wide tonal range equivalent to 10 f-stops (this is similar to negative film and much wider than standard reversal film which can only record a tonal range of 6 f-stops) in practice detail tends to be lost in shadow areas if an exposure is set to preserve highlight detail. To rectify this use silver bounce cards and focus them on any dark shadow areas which you think might fill in.

Fourthly underexposed images can be 'pushed', as with film, by amplifying the image data; tonal range is reduced as in film but an image's resolution remains constant.

Royalty based

Comstock	Numerous subjects
Corbis	Arts and recreation, science and industry, natural world, travel and culture...
Hulton Getty	Historical photographs...
The Telegraph Colour Library	Numerous subjects
Tony Stone Images	Numerous subjects
Untitled	X-rayed items...

Contact numbers in UK: Comstock 0171 351 4448; Corbis 0171 843 4444
Hulton Getty 0171 266 2662; The Telegraph Colour Library 0171 293 2929;
Tony Stone Images 0171 544 3333; Untitled 01474 815004

Royalty free

Artbeats	Textures...
Artville	Illustrations...
Andromeda	Maps...
Cartesia	Maps...
Central Stock	Antique maps, people, textures...
Diamar	Backgrounds, people...
Digital Media	Objects...
Digital Stock	Numerous subjects
Digital Vision	Numerous subjects
Focoltone	Textures...
Imagin	Architecture, landscape, textures...
John Foxx images	Hi-tech, business, nature, people...
PhotoDisc	Objects, people, business...
PhotoAlto	Landscapes, textures...
Photo Essentials	Nature, people, objects, business...
Stockbyte	Numerous subjects
Scorpius	Agriculture, business, textures
Slides Pro	Textures, women...
Signs 2000	Signs...
StockPix	Families, couples, children...
Thomstock Unidisc	Occupations, people, nature...
Ultimate Symbol	Motifs...
Visual Language	Antique maps...

Suppliers in UK: Cadmium Systems Freephone 0800 436867; Presentation Direct
Freephone 0800 969696

Originators: Digital Stock: 800 545 4514 (USA); PhotoDisc: Freephone 0800
697622; Stockbyte: Freephone 0800 909190

Table 4.3 Some image sources

Creating informative diagrams

Diagrams give visual expression to abstract facts and functions which cannot effectively be depicted by other means.

To be effective they need to be both informative and aesthetically pleasing. Their data needs to be organised, distilled and transformed in a rational manner yet their visual form needs to be graphically appealing to enhance communication.

Thus the right balance of aesthetics and information value is crucial for success. This presents a design challenge as no matter how interesting a diagram might look, unless it communicates effectively and is in an appropriate graphic style it will fail as a piece of information design.

Main types of diagram:

- statistical diagrams, such as pie and bar charts
- flow diagrams (such as diagrams describing manufacturing production), organisation charts, time charts
- diagrams visualising functions and processes
- tabulations and timetables
- cartographic diagrams and decorative maps
- diagrams used as design elements

Creating diagrams

You can create diagrams from scratch within a draw program or you can use diagram creation tools which automate the production process. Such tools are available in Microsoft Excel, Adobe Illustrator or as separate dedicated programs.

Using a diagram creation tool obviously saves time but the results, if unmodified, often look run-of-the-mill. This may be fine for a functional internal management document but not one aimed at a wider audience. In the latter case it's best to restrict such tools to doing the basic building work and modify results to create designs of your choosing.

Statistical diagrams are perhaps the most common type of diagram and there are many tools available to transform data into graph types such as pie, bar and scatter. Flow diagrams, organisation charts, time charts and diagrams visualising functions and processes are also widely used. Again, there are charting tools available which can generate some of these from data.

Tabulations and timetables can either be treated in a diagrammatic way or be integrated into diagrams and for this reason I include them in my list. Cartographic diagrams and decorative maps are further types which can take many forms. An interesting problem arises when working on political maps where countries that share a border of positive length (not just isolated points) are required to have different colours. In fact, four colours suffice to meet this requirement, but it was only in 1976 that this was proved by mathematicians.

Finally, diagrams can be used as design elements, e.g. a diagram can be used, in stripped-down form, as a front cover design for a company brochure or can be used as part of a corporate identity device.

Perspective and projections

What perspective or projection system should one use within diagrams? Of course, that depends on many factors, including:

- the level of information you need to convey
- the amount of suitable reference material you have at hand
- your construction skills, e.g. diagrams drawn in true perspective are more difficult to construct than plans and elevations
- the amount of time you can devote to a diagram

Out of all the options available to the illustrator, three-dimensional objects are often best drawn using axonometric projections. They are relatively easy to construct as they are based on a plan view, they present 3-D properties quite well and they have a technical feel about them which the more natural three-point perspective lacks. Most graphing programs use this type of projection to construct bar charts for these very reasons. Of course, many graphic devices are two dimensional and so standard orthographic projection suffices.

Orthographic projection

Orthographic projection is the simplest form of projection consisting solely of plans, elevations and sections. But unlike other forms it does not convey 3-D properties very well. To visualise complicated forms from such projections is no mean task.

Axonometric projections

Illustrations drawn using axonometric projections convey the 3-D properties of subjects extremely well and like orthographic projections they can represent all dimensions to scale. Such projections clarify form, construction and design but are not pure geometry but a convention (Fig. 4.35).

Right angles (in the orthographic plan view) usually remain right angles in the axonomeric view but are rotated at the most suitable angle, usually 45°/45°, 50°/40° and 60°/30°. In all cases the vertical dimensions are to the same scale as the rotated plan. When the two angles are equal, as in a 45°/45° projection, they are termed isometric.

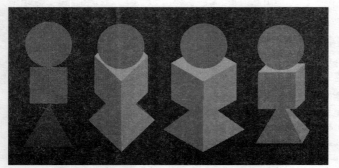

Fig. 4.35 An elevation and various axonometric projections

Three-point perspective

Three-point perspective is the most natural of perspective projections. The fundamentals of this method are best explained by means of a cube. By visualising an object suspended within the cube it will follow that its perspective will be the same as the cube.

Three sets of vanishing lines are involved in the cube's construction: one set of four vertical lines connecting its corners and two horizontal sets, one forming its top edges, the other its bottom edges.

Digitising images

Before any images can be used within DTP documents, they need to be in digital format – to be 'electronically' bitmapped. If they are not, they will need to be scanned. Images from photo libraries, captured by digital cameras or created within a draw or paint program will already be digital. In these cases, scanning is not required.

Bitmapped images of all types usually need to be enhanced to improve their tones, colours and sharpness or to bring them more into line with a vision of how you wish them to look on the page. Some images may go through further processes to give them special effects or to prepare them for integration into a montage.

Obtaining good scans

The quality of bitmapped images – their sharpness, tonal range, colour values, level of detail, etc. – very much depends on the data recorded during the scanning process (Fig. 4.36). No amount of post-scanning image editing can make up for inadequacy in this area. Improvements can be made and some weaknesses addressed but the result will never match up to the original if it had been scanned properly in the first place.

The quality of originals is also crucial for success as it represents the base-point for the bitmapped data. One can't reasonably expect perfect results if originals are poor in the first place. It doesn't matter too much what form originals are in – colour transparencies, photographic prints, printed material or flat artwork are all scannable.

Fig. 4.36 Close-up of photographic original and scan (both much enlarged)

However, as a general rule masters are superior to prints or copies, e.g. transparencies are preferable to colour prints as the latter have been generated from the former and as a consequence are slightly degraded.

Obtaining the optimum amount of recorded data to ensure good reproduction depends on many factors, not least the setting of the correct mode, resolution and dimensions for a given subject.

The scanning mode is usually determined by the level of colour you wish to have in a final image; image dimensions depend on the size at which you wish to use an image and resolution depends on outputting or retouching factors.

Continuous tone and line subjects demand different scanning approaches, depending on the bit-depth you require.

Continuous tone images

For continuous tone subjects resolution should always be based on the pitch of the halftone screen used for the final outputting device (whether it is digital or analogue) and the dimensions should match the final printed size.

Graphic motifs, such as colour logotypes and symbols, often need to be scanned at a higher resolution than you finally plan to use so that their design properties can be more easily fine-tuned by post-scanning editing work.

The correct shadow, highlight and gamma setup is also crucial for success if scans are to contain sufficient detail at all tonal levels.

Fig. 4.37 Close-up of a line subject scanned in grayscale (much enlarged)

Line images

1-bit images tend to break up edges and reduce linear detail, so their scanned resolution needs to be as high as possible, but no more than twice your scanner's optical resolution at 100 per cent scale. (I discuss the optimum production resolution for line work later in this section.)

Surprisingly, finely detailed subjects are better scanned in grayscale rather than in line and only converted once tonal levels have been adjusted within an image editing program (Fig. 4.37). Manual adjustment is preferable to automatic settings as you are able to decide which levels of grey convert to white or black rather than leaving it to a machine to decide. A further benefit from scanning in grayscale is that images can be rotated by small amounts. In line mode, rotations are strictly limited to 90° increments.

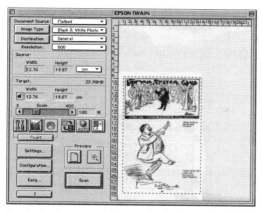

Fig. 4.38 Epson well-designed TWAIN scanning controls

Ways of setting image sizes

It's normally best to scan to final dimensions and resolution rather than adjust these attributes later, except for the cases mentioned earlier. However, you can, if you wish, scan at 100 per cent or other scale at a resolution which takes into account any later rescaling (Fig. 4.38).

If you do this you will need to increase an image's scanned resolution by the same factor as you are going to increase its scale, i.e. if you plan to double an image's dimensions, you need roughly to double its scanned resolution.

Examples:

Scanned resolution/dimensions
600 ppi/150×105 mm
300 ppi/65×100 mm

Final resolution/dimensions
300/300×210 mm
150 ppi/130×200 mm

Sometimes your scanner's controls will force you to work in this manner. Some transmissive scanners, notably those made by Kodak, include neither a dimension field nor a resolution field. The amount of data in a scan is set by an image size control. Images are always scanned at 72 ppi to dimensions set by this control. Once scanned, images can be altered to the required resolution and dimensions within an image editing program such as Photoshop or enlarged within a page layout or draw program.

Colour modes

Scanning terminology can be confusing to beginners as different manufacturers use different words to describe the same things, especially the level of colour (mode) of images. This attribute can be variously described as:

- 1-bit; line; bitmap; bilevel: black and white
- 8-bit; grayscale: black and white photo
- 24-bit; colour: millions of colours
- 30-bit; 48-bit; colour: billions of colours

1-bit refers to images which contain only black and white areas; 8-bit refers to images which contain 256 shades of grey, including black and white; 24-bit refers to images which contain over 16.7 million colours; both 30-bit and 48-bit refer to images which contain billions of colours.

The terms line, black and white photo and colour refer to the type of originals normally recorded for the given bit-depths.

Choosing image resolutions

Continuous tone images

Continuous tone (grayscale and colour) images, by definition, contain graduations and therefore need to be screened when output to print.

Screening is necessary as most printing technologies are not intrinsically tonal, i.e. areas of their printing surfaces are either fully inked or free from ink – there's no in-between condition. (See Chapter 5.)

The traditional and most widely used method of screening is called halftoning (Fig. 4.39). This method involves converting tonal and colour values into a grid of dots of varying sizes. As the grid or screen is relatively fine the eye merges the dots and intervening spaces to give a sensation of tonal and colour variety.

A more recent innovation is dithered 'screenless' printing, such as stochastic screening. This involves scattering microdots in a controlled way across the area of an image. These dots are often no bigger than a device's machine dots. The relationship of the dots to white space gives the necessary data for the sensation of tonal and colour variety.

These dithered screens combine very high tonal range with image sharpness and for this very reason they are likely to be used increasingly on both digital printers and printing presses as the technology becomes more widespread.

Halftone screens are normally measured in lines per inch (lpi) and can be as low as 80 lpi for grayscale images in newspapers and as high as 200 lpi for colour images in art books.

It is the final printing device and paper stock which determine the pitch of the halftone screen. In turn the halftone screen determines image resolution.

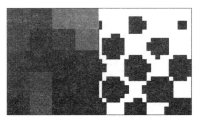

Fig. 4.39 Close-up of an image: (left) as pixels and (right) as a halftone made up of machine dots (both much enlarged)

Ideally the resolution of your image should be roughly twice-linear the halftone screen setting of your final printing device, i.e. if your final printing device is a digital printer and its halftone screen is set at 60 lpi then the resolution of your image should be 120 ppi (dpi) or thereabouts.

Most offset-litho work will be screened at between 100 and 200 lpi, the exact pitch depending on the surface smoothness of the paper to be printed on. Silkscreen work will usually be screened at no more than 100 lpi. Your printing company will be able to advise you on the appropriate halftone screen ruling for specific jobs.

If you are scanning images for temporary use only and you plan to replace the images later in the production process, the image resolution need only be 72 ppi (dpi). This will give you acceptable on-screen display and basic proof quality whilst keeping file sizes to the minimum.

If you are outputting using a stochastic or other type of dithered screen set the image resolution to roughly one-third of the device's outputting resolution.

If your printing device prints in continuous tone set the image resolution to match the device's outputting resolution, which will probably be between 300 and 400 ppi (dpi).

It's not normally necessary to take into account an imagesetter's resolution when establishing resolutions for grayscale and colour images as it is an intermediary device. However, an imagesetter's resolution does affect tonal values in halftones so its setting needs to be considered when reproducing images requiring the widest tonal range.

Number of levels of grey in a halftone:

Halftone screen	Resolution of machine dots			
	300 dpi	600 dpi	1200 dpi	2540 dpi
75 lpi	17	65	256	256
100 lpi	10	37	145	256
150 lpi	5	17	65	256

The same principle applies to digital presses, except that on some devices the amount of ink or toner applied can be varied on a dot by dot basis. This technique, called variable dot density, gives extremely detailed shading, good colour graduation and high image sharpness.

Line images

Line images don't require screening as they lack tonal variation, so their resolutions should be based on your digital printer's resolution or, in the case of work going to press, the imagesetter's resolution, e.g. if your digital printer's resolution is 600 dpi, the resolution of your line image should be as high as possible but no higher than 600 ppi (dpi). Imagesetters output at 1270 or 2540 dpi, so resolutions tend to be between 600 and 1270 dpi.

Enhancing images

What is it that makes some images work on the page and others not? Why do some images leap out at you whilst others are hardly noticeable. What is it that determines image quality?

Undoubtedly key depictive qualities – such as viewing angle, focus, exposure time, composition with the frame – contribute much to the power of an image, indeed often more so than the subject itself. A professional photographer can make even the most mundane subject come alive through the skilful manipulation of such attributes.

Fig. 4.40 Tonal and special effects. The same image inverted, embossed, posterised and spherized

Photographers will tell you that they paint with light. This is quite correct. Photographs are records of light – with light, shade and colour being their essential qualities.

These qualities, the product of lens, shutter and emulsion/CCD matrix, form a photograph's visual grammar and it's through their manipulation that images can be altered to suit the purpose in hand. The manipulation may be routine, such as the fine-tuning of tonal values, or it may be more involved. Further work may be necessary for a number of reasons:

- to match tonal and colour values in images to their subjects
- to harmonise tonal and colour values in a range of images to give them artistic unity
- to express a vision of how the images should look, which may differ greatly from how they really are

Focus, tones and colours

Whilst I suggest general rules for achieving good image quality, they are not intended to be applicable in all situations. Common sense will tell you which of the following points are relevant to the image at hand, e.g. a scan of a very old photograph will lose a great deal of character if you make 'improvements' which aren't symphathetic. Part of the charm and quality of old images derives from their limited tonal range and artificial colouring and such attributes should be carefully maintained if authenticity is desired.

Therefore, as a general rule:

- images should not be too grainy or spotty or too blurred
- tones in images should be neither too bleached out nor too sooty
- a full tonal range should be represented, including both black and white points
- tones in images should be neither too flat nor too contrasty
- images should not have a colour cast, i.e. too much red or yellow, nor should they appear weak or over-rich

Removing noise and sharpening

It is preferable that images should be correctly focused and free from 'noise'. This usually means that the focus is sharp but in some cases it may mean that a soft focus is maintained. The appropriate level of sharpness depends on many factors, not least the proposed printing process.

Noise – moirés, dottiness, etc. – is invariably unsightly and should be minimised where possible. In contrast photographic grain, being an intrinsic feature of photographic enlargements, is desirable and should be maintained within a scan, especially if an image is soft in focus.

Removing noise

High levels of noise within an image can often be avoided if sharpening is disabled during scanning. Also, descreen filters are useful for minimising the effect of halftone screens within printed material. Both settings usually result in a softer, less focused image but this can easily be rectified after scanning.

However, should noise still be present in a scanned image, it can be minimised or removed using a despeckle or gaussian blur filter. Both soften an image, so sharpening is usually required after their use.

Increasing edge definition

Most images need edge sharpening for good reproduction. This is because halftoning and 'screenless' printing methods, such as stochastic screening, represent edges as dots on final printed matter. This effectively reduces the definition between forms within images.

Library images, such as those stored in Kodak Photo CD format, particularly need sharpening as they are intentionally supplied slightly soft, particularly when opened at maximum resolution. This is because any edge sharpening inevitably and irrecovably alters an image and limits its usefulness.

Sharpening is achieved by using either a standard sharpening filter or an unsharp mask. The former tends to give a gritty effect to images – they become 'noisier' as the contrast between pixels is increased whether they represent edges or not. This may not be a problem if an image is very soft in the first place. However an increase in noise is usually undesirable so the use of an unsharp mask is preferred. Despite its name, unsharp mask improves sharpness by increasing edge contrast. It over-emphasises the tonal difference at edges creating a kind of halo effect.

As a general rule, when sharpening images as part of an enhancement process edges viewed on screen at print size should look sharp without appearing artificial. However, when sharpening images as part of a pre-press adjustment edges viewed at print size should look oversharp, with obvious edge artefacts.

Adjusting tones

Most images should have a good breadth of tones ranging from black in the shadow areas through to white in the highlight areas. Midtones should be neither too dark nor too light and the level of contrast should be appropriate.

Setting black and white points

The darkest and lightest tones in an image dictate an image's tonal breadth. The presence of true blacks and whites contribute to an image's dramatic appeal, and this applies to both high- and low-key subjects – images with predominately light or dark tones.

However, the absence of blacks and whites in images which rely on subtle tonal passages for their atmosphere – misty subjects, night-time subjects and so on – may sometimes be appropriate.

Adjusting the tonal breadth of images involves either making the darkest tones black and the lightest tones white (Fig. 4.41) or selecting tones that represent specific image areas and setting the points from these. By selecting specific areas, the tonal breadth is not dictated by arbitrary values.

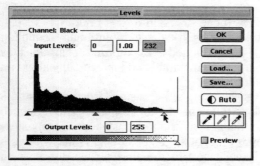

Fig. 4.41 Setting the black and white points in Photoshop

Selecting the right areas is often a matter of common sense and involves looking at an image closely and deciding which aspects of the subject are important, e.g. if an image portrays a man in a dark suit and the man is the key subject (from an editorial point of view) then look for a very dark area in a fold of his jacket, and a very light area on his shirt cuff. Set the white and black points from these areas and gauge the effect.

Because the eye tends to be drawn to the brightest areas within an image, setting the correct white point is probably more important than setting the black. Certainly, by selecting points yourself you are effectively controlling how you wish an image to be 'read' and this must be better than leaving it to chance.

Setting midtone brightness

The values of midtones – the tones which are in neither the darkest nor the lightest ranges – affect an image's perceived brightness. If the midtones appear too dark detail may be lost and if they are appear too light an image may look washed out.

Adjusting brightness involves darkening or lightening an image whilst ensuring that neither its black nor white points are affected.

Adjusting contrast

The contrast of an image determines its tonal intensity or tonality.

High-contrast images tend to have intense blacks and whites, often adjacent to one another, with a limited range of intermediate tones. An extreme example of this is silhouettes. Low-contrast images, on the other hand, have pervading grey tones with blacks and whites less in evidence. Tones tend to graduate rather than contrast and they rely on delicacy of atmosphere for their dramatic charge.

Unfortunately excessively high-contrast images can appear sooty. This effect can be reduced by flattening tones – making the images less contrasty – but adjustments are usually unsatisfactory as shadow and/or highlight values often lack the necessary tonal detail. Low-contrast images, on the other hand, can seem too flat even though a full range of tones may be present. An increase in contrast makes them punchier, albeit at the expense of some tonal loss in shadow and highlight areas but this does not generally present a problem.

In colour images, juxtaposed complementary colours can provide contrast independently of tonal value. Images containing such contrasts are less reliant on tonal distinction for their success.

Balancing colours

Colour images that are balanced appear natural; when unbalanced they have a colour cast, i.e. some or all of their colours are tinged to a greater or lesser extent by a single hue, such as blue. The resulting effect, if marked, can make an image look quite surreal. This may or may not be acceptable from a creative point of view.

Colour casts are caused by a number of factors:

- a mismatch between film type and lighting
- the use of lense filters
- overexposure or non-standard film processing
- coloured lighting in a subject

The use of daylight film with tungsten light will give an image a yellowy-orange cast and with fluorescent light a green cast, whereas tungsten film shot in daylight gives a strong blue cast. If either film type is used in mixed lighting conditions, the resulting cast may be localised unless corrective lens filters are used.

Casts can also be caused by coloured lamps, light filtered through coloured materials or reflected off coloured surfaces such as wall coverings, and they can be image-wide or localised, depending on the set-up.

Casts may be intentional or unintentional. In some images a cast may be the key to their emotive appeal, whereas in others they may rightly be perceived as a technical fault. This may not matter in some cases since casts, being often present in photographs, are accepted as a legitimate part of a photograph's visual makeup.

Casts can be removed by adjusting the proportion of the problem colour in an image. The same technique is used to intensify an image's mood or atmosphere by cooling or warming its colours.

If casts are localised, corrections can be made by restricting adjustments to specific colours, such as skin tones, colours in certain tonal ranges such as highlights, or particular passages within an image. Masks or selective colour controls are used for such retrictive adjustment.

The colour wheel

Rebalancing colours is perhaps the hardest type of adjustment to make, as it requires not only good colour perception but an understanding of the way colours interact with each other.

The colour wheel shows the relationship of component colours in a colour image (Fig. 4.42). Notice that equal proportions of red and blue make magenta, equal proportions of blue and green make cyan and equal proportions of green and red make yellow.

Of course, the whole gamut of hues (all the colours in the rainbow) should really be shown around the wheel, from red, violet, indigo, blue, green, yellow, through to orange and back to red again.

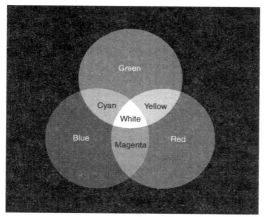

Fig. 4.42 The colour wheel, showing the additive colours, red, blue and green, mixing to create the subtractive colours, cyan, magenta and yellow

The colour balance

Colour balance is best explained by referring to a graphic balance with red, green and blue weights (Fig. 4.43).

When colours are unbalanced, images will have a preponderance of a hue, such as red. To correct the imbalance you need to alter the strength of the problem colour.

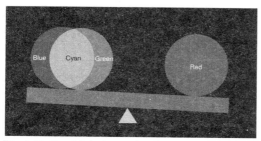

Fig. 4.43 Graphic balance showing cyan, made up of blue and green, slightly out of balance with red

You can do this by reducing the problem colour itself, in this case red, or by strengthening the complementary colour, in this case cyan (or both green and blue which make up cyan, if cyan is not represented by a control).

When a colour is strengthened or reduced it alters the proportion of opposing colours; because of this interaction usually only fine adjustments are necessary.

Adjusting saturation

The saturation of an image determines the cleanliness or otherwise of its constituent colours. When colours are low in saturation they are greyed. In photographs this can be caused by dull lighting conditions, hazes and mists and the use of long focal lenses. When colours are highly saturated, the opposite occurs; the grey component of colours is minimal so they appear over-rich and artificial.

Drab-looking images can often benefit from a slight increase in saturation to inject a bit of life into them whilst perfectly good images may be heavily desaturated to give a subtle, colour-wash effect thereby enhancing their dramatic appeal.

The degree to which colours are greyed affects the mood of an image so it's important to set saturation values at appropriate levels.

Cropping and cutting around images

Cropping

Skilful cropping enhances most photographs. It can improve the composition of a weakly structured image and show off a well-composed image to its best.

Cropping also enables you to focus on and develop a theme using only part of an image, e.g. an area can be selected for its colours to evoke a particular mood or to create semi-abstract effects.

The proportion of a crop often entails a compromise between what works for the image and what works in layout terms. For instance, the use of a modular grid system will dictate the proportions available to you; it may be that none of them are absolutely right for a particular image.

Images can be cropped during the scanning process, cropped again within an image manipulation program and/or within a host draw or page layout document.

Within a scanner's controls or within a program, such as Photoshop, cropping reduces the overall image area. Cropping within a draw or page layout program simply masks off parts of an image. The image is viewed as though through a window. It's a simple job therefore to reposition an image relative to its window and/or to alter its scale and thus its crop.

Cutouts

You can cut out parts of an image so that its background becomes completely transparent (Fig. 4.44). This is a useful technique if you wish to overlay images within pages as any underlying elements show around their shaped edges.

Cutouts act as an effective visual foil to rectangular images but they are also a useful way of eliminating unsightly backgrounds.

Cutouts are usually achieved by means of clipping paths. These mask out areas of grayscale and colour images which normally would be opaque, even in their white areas. Of course, if an image is not going to overlay other images, transparency is not an issue and a clipping path is not required. In that case it's then only necessary to white out non-printing areas you wish to appear blank.

Clipping paths can be added directly to bitmapped images within Photoshop or indirectly within a draw program, such as Illustrator, or a page layout program, such as QuarkXPress.

Fig. 4.44 Clipping path allowing underlying type to show within the rectangular confines of the overlying image

Montaging and special effects

Montaging

Montages provide an interesting way of communicating multiple ideas within a single image (Fig. 4.45). Because of their composite nature they are perfect for telling a story, for projecting complex visual concepts and conveying interrelated ideas; they can also be used to trick the eye into thinking the image represents reality.

Montaging is normally achieved within image manipulation programs. These programs allow you to combine different images within a single document and to modify them at will.

Ruler guides and user-adjustable grids assist in accurate image positioning.

Montaging work invariably involves the clipboard. In Photoshop this feature is directly linked to the layers function. Pasted images are automatically placed on transparent layers of their own. This allows you to alter the attributes of pasted images before merging them with other images or artwork.

Layers are an extremely important Photoshop feature. They enable you to experiment freely with complex montages without you having to create separate versions of documents. They also allow you to test and apply image graduations and other effects easily with their layer mask function.

Fig. 4.45 A montaged image created by combining several scans in one document

Layered Photoshop documents can only be saved in their native file formats, which usually can't be imported by other programs. When an image is ready for use, you save a flattened copy in a format of your choice or flatten the image you are working in.

Special effects

Special effects can be applied to bitmapped and vector images, and range from simple textural treatments to outlandish distortions. Those that have the most impact tend to be the simpler and more subtle ones. Convoluted effects have gimmick value but can be tiresome if overused.

The simpler effects have as their antecedents traditional photographic darkroom processes (Fig. 4.40). Such effects include posterisation, solarisation, bas reliefs, line conversions and sepia/duotoning. The more complex effects are the products of computer modelling.

The programs that create special effects are provided in the form of extensions or modules which are either bundled with draw and bitmap programs or supplied as separate products. Such products include Adobe Gallery Effects, Alien Skin TextureShop, Andromeda Series, Kai's Power Tools, KPT Convolver, Paint Alchemy, Sucking Fish Filters and Terrazzo.

Collating your own images

The more illustrated documents you produce, the more images you will accumulate. Even with the most organised filing regime, there will inevitably become a time when image retrieval becomes a nightmare.

There are a number of utilities on the market designed to get round the problem. These programs create catalogues of DTP files which can then be organised, searched, annotated and previewed as required.

Cumulus, a leading cataloguing software made by Canto, works by holding references to the location of files, not the files themselves, so that images can be stored on remote servers or removable disks and don't have to clog your internal drive. When you wish to retrieve a file that is not on your main drive, you are requested to mount a server/removable disk as required.

A catalogue is created by dragging a folder or disk into Cumulus which will then create thumbnails (small, low-resolution images) of all the images it contains, recording salient aspects of each file including file type, size, resolution and creator program.

The catalogue is broken down into organised categories for easy searching, allowing you either to use the file path in a hierarchical manner or to define your own categories and physically assign files by dragging and dropping thumbnails onto as many category icons as you wish.

Ways of working with bitmapped images

Unlike vector images, bitmapped images have large file sizes, which can create storage problems. However, there are several practices that you can adopt if you lack sufficient storage capacity. One is to import roughly scanned, low-resolution images into your documents. These images will be good enough to work with and will give an indication to all concerned of the required treatment and positioning of images.

After you have completed your documents, accurately scanned, high-resolution versions of these images can be substituted for the low-resolution ones, whether you are planning to imageset your documents or just wish to have the best possible printing quality. The advantage of this approach is that you avoid having to store large picture files on your system and you can leave the accurate scanning work to others.

This basic idea has been incorporated into a system called Open Press Interface (OPI), a sophisticated process of image duplication and file substitution used for the imagesetting of large documents involving many images.

Another practice is simply not to import bitmapped images; just create boxes and frame them. The printed frames indicate where the images should go and you supply your bureau with the original transparencies and prints and tell them which image goes where and how each is to be sized and cropped.

Inserting images
When you import scanned and vectored images into a page layout document, either low-resolution bitmapped versions of the original images are embedded within the document or images are embedded at high-resolution.

In the case of low-resolution images being embedded, links are established between the embedded images and their originals. When you output your document, the page layout program takes the data detailing the positioning, scaling and cropping of the embedded images and applies it to the original images, which are then used in place of the low-resolution images.

Linking images to documents

On both Macintosh and Windows systems, images can be linked to documents in such a way that the separation between document and image is reduced to the minimum.

These linking technologies, unique to each system, allow you to dynamically edit and update information without the need manually to locate and open individual imported images. This saves you a great deal of time especially if many images are involved in a document and you wish to repeatedly revisit and update the images as you work.

The Macintosh system is called Publish and Subscribe; Windows' is called Object Linking and Embedding (OLE). Each system uses it own terminology; the Macintosh uses a publishing metaphor whilst Windows uses a client/server metaphor. The systems work in a similar way although OLE gives you the option of embedding copies of 'client' images within the 'server' document.

Publish and Subscribe

Publish and Subscribe creates an active link between a graphic (or scan or text) file and a host document (such as a QuarkXPress document). Source images (such as Illustrator documents) are 'published' creating Edition files. It is these Edition files that are 'subscribed to' by the host documents.

Such images can be moved, copied and multiply-pasted elsewhere within the document in the same way as if they had been imported by any other method.

Object Linking and Embedding

Object Linking and Embedding creates an active link between a graphic object within a 'server' document and a 'client' document. Server images are pasted into client documents in one of two ways: either a link is established or a copy of the full image is embedded.

Both the server program and the client program must be running at the same time for the server documents to open. In the case of embedding, the server program automatically launches itself when needed and does not have to be operating in advance.

Which is better: to link an image or to embed it?

Linking is better if you wish subsequent changes in a server document to be reflected in many client documents. This is possible because the server document is the original file and is completely independent of any client document.

On the other hand, embed if you wish subsequent changes in a server document to be reflected only in the client document in which it is embedded. This is possible because the server document is a duplicate of the original file and is not linked to any other client documents.

Deciding on which file format to use

The multitude of graphic file formats confuses many new to desktop publishing. Yet an understanding of the various types and their specific uses is essential if you wish to import images into documents and successfully output them as part of page layout documents.

A file format is the way an image, or other data, is stored in a file. The way it is stored will determine not only how much disk space the file will take up, but its specification and the use that can be made of an image (Fig. 4.46).

For example, a TIFF file has a relatively large file size, can store millions of colours and be accepted by most programs, whilst a PICT file is compact, can also store millions of colours but can't hold data in CMYK mode.

Some file formats employ compression algorithms to reduce file sizes on disk. TIFF features the LZW algorithm whilst JPEG has its own system. The LZW system keeps data intact whilst JPEG decimates data to achieve its high compression levels.

The main formats

Most scanned and drawn images to be imported into documents should be saved in TIFF, EPS, JPEG, Photo CD, Photoshop, PICT, BMP or PCX formats. Page layout documents are usually saved in their native formats, such as PageMaker 7 or QuarkXPress 4, although in the future more and more of these host documents will probably be distilled into PDF format.

TIFF

Scanned images are often saved in TIFF (Tagged Image File Format). This format was originally developed by Microsoft and Aldus and has become a standard worldwide. It can be used to save bilevel, grayscale, RGB images up to 48-bit and CMYK images in 24-bit.

TIFF files do not embed themselves within a document – they're tagged – so you need to keep the original files for outputting purposes.

EPS

Vectored drawn images are usually saved in Encapsulated PostScript (EPS), as are scanned images containing PostScript elements. This format was originally developed by Altsys; it is generic and comes in many forms. Drawings produced in Macromedia FreeHand and Adobe Illustrator, for instance, are saved in this format. It can be used to save bilevel, grayscale, RGB and CMYK colour images in 24-bit.

Like TIFF files, EPS files do not embed themselves within your document so you need to keep the original files for outputting purposes. As they are substantially larger than TIFFs – about a third again in size – it's best to avoid this format for bitmapped images unless you really need its features.

JPEG

Scanned images are often saved in JPEG (Joint Photographic Experts Group) format. This format was developed for the newspaper publishing industry and has become a worldwide standard for transmitting images by modem. It can be used to save bilevel, grayscale, RGB and CMYK colour images in 24-bit.

Because this file format decimates data it's not recommended for normal production work.

Photo CD

This format is specific to Kodak and at present cannot be used to save images onto Macintoshes and PCs. There are several versions of Photo CD but the main one is Master Photo CD for 35 mm. It's used to save YCC colour images in 24-bit, in an image pack of five different resolutions.

Photoshop (native)

Scans can be saved in native Photoshop file format. This format is native to Photoshop although some programs have recently been able to import images saved this way. There are several versions of

Photoshop: 2.0, 2.5, 3.0, 4.0 and 5.0. It can be used to save bilevel, grayscale and RGB images up to 48-bit and CMYK in 24-bit.

It is worth noting that later versions of the program can open earlier versions but not the other way round.

PICT File

Vectored drawings/charts and scans can be saved in PICT. This is Apple's native format and it uses the same routines as the software that draws the Macintosh screen. It can be used to save bilevel, grayscale and RGB colour images up to 24-bit.

PICT files always embed themselves in their entirety within the document so you don't need to keep the original files for output.

File format	RGB	CMYK 24-bit	Grayscale 8-bit	Bilevel 1-bit
TIFF	●	●	●	●
Photoshop EPS	●	●	●	●
JPEG	●	●	●	
Photo CD				
Photoshop (native)	●	●	●	●
PICT File	●		●	●
BMP	●		●	●
PCX	●		●	●
PDF	●		●	

Fig. 4.46 File formats and colour support

BMP

Scans can be saved in BMP (Windows Bitmap). This is Windows' native Paint format. It can be used to save bilevel, grayscale and RGB images in 24-bit.

PCX

Scans can be saved in PCX (Windows Bitmap). This is an old DOS PC Paintbrush format which is available in a number of versions. It can be used to save bilevel, grayscale and RGB in 24-bit.

PDF

Whole documents can be saved in PDF (Portable Document Format). This format was developed by Adobe to meet the need for a single compact, device- and media-independent file which could be viewed and output on different and often remote devices without requiring originating programs, special print drivers or printer description files. PostScript pages, fonts, colours and vector and bitmapped images are faithfully saved.

———————— Using colour ————————

Used well, colour is one of desktop publishing's most powerful resources. It brings documents to life by infusing them with a special quality not attainable by other means.

Colour can enrich documents in all sorts of ways: it can evoke a particular mood, make a style statement, support a corporate identity or act as a coding device. Whatever its purpose, it rarely fails to make documents more attractive to the reader.

Since colour can have such an impact on the way documents are perceived, it's worth learning about what colour is, how it's modelled and how it's managed within desktop publishing programs.

What is colour?

Colour and perception

The rainbow is a useful starting point when discussing colour as it is nature's way of showing off the full range of hues visible – violet, indigo, blue, green, yellow, orange and red. These are the spectral colours, with each colour representing a different electromagnetic frequency. White light is made up of all these colours in equal amounts and of course darkness is an absence of all colours.

Whilst colour represents the visible part of the electromagnetic spectrum, it is purely a sensation. The human eye and brain 'sees' by means of photosensitive red, green and blue cones. It is through the cones' responses to the electromagnetic waves and the subsequent processing of the data within the brain that we are able to sense and thus to distinguish between the colours we see around us.

As the brain takes into account the whitest and blackest points of the subject in view, the perceived tonal gamut of the subject is continually adjusted. The eye is forever referencing tonal limits to optimise the mapping of colours in the brain and thereby give a balanced and representative colour sensation.

Interestingly some colours, such as browns and metallics, cannot be fully sensed by the photosensitive cones. Knowledge of an object's identity, the complexity of its surface texture, the presence of colour contrasts, and changes of angle; all play their part in helping the eye and brain see such colours.

Biological and psychological factors unique to individuals play their part in determining how colour is perceived. Because everyone's brain is unique, colour data is processed slightly differently. As a result colour perception is highly subjective.

Reflected light

Most of the light that reaches our eyes starts off as white light. When it strikes an object, the object's surface absorbs certain ranges of wavelengths and reflects others. Consequently the reflected light contains a different mixture of wavelengths of light to that of white light. It is this mixture which gives an object its colour. Our perception of colour therefore depends very much on how an object attenuates light waves.

The colour of light

The colour of light sources is measured in kelvins (K). When an object is heated to increasing temperatures, it emits light ranging from red, orange, yellow, white through to blue. It is the direct relationship between the temperature of an incandescent object and the colour of the light it gives off that enables light to be described in terms of its temperature. Morning and evening daylight are around 5,000 K and an overcast sky is near 6,250 K.

Mixing colours

Colours are mixed in desktop publishing by one of two means. One is based on light, the other on inks. The first is known as additive colour and is employed by scanners and monitors. The second is known as subtractive colour and is employed by printing devices.

Either way colours are defined using colour spaces (sometimes called colour models), of which RGB, CMYK, HSB and Hexachrome are examples. CIE Yxy and L*a*b* colour models, devised in 1931 and 1976 respectively by the Commission Internationale de l'Eclairage, provide a fundamental referencing point for these and other colour spaces used in desktop publishing.

Colour gamuts

Just as the perception of colour varies from individual to individual, each device in the desktop publishing process relies on a different method of imaging colour. The different technologies – CCD, phosphors, inkjet and such like – limit the number of colours that can be recorded, displayed or output.

Thus the gamut of colours available at any one time to the desktop publisher is determined not only by the colour space employed but by the technology of the device.

A scanner RGB, monitor RGB, offset press CMYK, offset press Hexachrome will therefore have different gamuts. This means that translation from one system to another inevitably leads to a colour shift.

Colour spaces explained

The number and types of colour spaces used within desktop publishing can be offputting to the beginner. But once you are familiar with what each space is used for and their advantages and disadvantages, you will soon understand the need for the different spaces.

In the main, desktop publishers work within RGB and CMYK colour spaces – RGB for scanning and displaying colour images and CMYK for colour printing. Both these spaces were designed to have a sufficiently wide gamut for colour illustrations and photographs.

Recently developed Hi-Fi colour spaces are likely to be used increasingly as an alternative to CMYK for certain types of printed document because of their wide colour gamuts. HSB, a colour space described in terms closer to how we perceive colour, is regularly employed for saturation adjustment.

The RGB colour space

Computer devices which use light as a medium, such as scanners and monitors, employ the RGB system. It's an additive system, with its three colours – red, green and blue – at full strength producing white light and at minimum strength leaving black. Equal strengths of each colour produce grey and unequal strengths create the hues in various degrees of brightness and saturation.

The CMYK colour space

Digital printing devices and conventional printing presses mostly use the four CMYK colours, known as the process colours. The exceptions include some low-end inkjet printers, some thermal wax transfer printers and some high-end proofing devices. Unlike the RGB colour space, this is a subtractive system, with its three colours – cyan, magenta, yellow – at medium strength producing near-black and all four colours at minimum strength leaving white. Black (the Key colour) is included in the model to provide a deep black not attainable by the colours alone because of impurities in inks.

Hi-Fi colour spaces
By involving six or more colours Hi-Fi colour spaces, such as Hexachrome, give a much wider colour gamut than the CMYK model. For example, by combining Hexachrome orange, green, cyan, magenta, yellow and black 90 per cent of the Pantone colour range can theoretically be matched (compared to less than 30 per cent using just CMYK inks). Potentially this makes images much more vivid and compelling.

Like CMYK Hi-Fi colour spaces are subtractive systems. Combinations of colours at medium strength produce near-black, and at minimum strength leave white. Black is usually included in these spaces to provide a deep black which would otherwise be unattainable.

Proprietary colour systems
Proprietary ink colours can also be printed on presses in addition to or instead of the CMYK colours. These colours are not intended to be mixed together. Instead they are normally used as spot colours for colouring illustrations, type and graphics and for duotones (grayscale images printed in two colours). Sometimes these systems are used for referencing only; their colours are converted to equivalent CMYK colours to avoid the need for additional printing plates. The Pantone Matching System (PMS) is probably the most widely used system of this type.

The YCC colour space
Kodak uses a further colour space for recording images on its Photo CDs. This system uses the YCC colours used for broadcasting TV signals. Two colour channels C and C combine with a monochrome channel Y.

The HSB colour space
The HSB colour space is closest to the way we, as humans, perceive colours, as distinct from how our eyes sense colours. Unlike other

spaces, which describe colours in terms of their constituent hues, HSB colours are described in a way which we can easily understand. Its three component properties are hue, saturation and brightness.

- *Hue* describes its spectral colour (red, green, yellow, etc.).
- *Saturation* describes its intensity or purity – the extent to which it is greyed (ranging from over-rich colour to colourless).
- *Brightness* describes its lightness or darkness – the extent to which it is whitened or blackened (ranging from very light to very dark).

Working with colour spaces

Since most DTP documents are destined for print, either CMYK, Hi-Fi or spot colours are finally specified. Bitmapped colour images all start off in RGB colour space and ideally should remain in this space until the images are ready for use. Any enhancement (including retouching, tonal and colour correction) and montaging can be done whilst images are in this space.

Not everyone follows this rule. Established colour reprographic houses prefer to convert their images to CMYK 'on the fly' during the scanning process. They do this because colour correction is specified along with other settings prior to scanning and not afterwards and they don't routinely get involved in other post-scanning work.

There are several advantages in keeping files in RGB mode:

- RGB file sizes are three-quarters of the size of CMYK files so they take up less memory – disk space and RAM
- RGB images have a broader colour gamut than CMYK images so there is more data available for image enhancement
- RGB images can be employed for uses other than for DTP, such as for web pages, since they retain their highly saturated colours

As with bitmapped images, vector images should be specified as either CMYK or spot. If they are integrated within a page layout program, usually the spot colours are automatically added to the host document's spot colour list.

Adding colour to documents

You can add colour to drawings and layouts either by applying colour to graphic elements and type or by importing coloured bitmapped and vector images.

Coloured bitmapped images need to be converted to CMYK before being imported into a document for final production.

Colours applied to type and graphics can be mixed using the CMYK colours or chosen from a proprietary colour system, such as PMS. Depending on the program you're working in, any colour, whatever its specification, can usually be delivered as either spot (sometimes called special or custom colour) or process.

Spot colours give you good colour fidelity but because each colour requires its own film separation and printing plate most jobs contain only one or two spot colours at most.

Process colours enable you to use almost a limitless number of colours but are generally only used if a document already contains full colour work (colour reproductions of photographs and/or illustrations) since CMYK films and plates will already be employed.

The issue of whether to specify spot or process is removed if you are outputting solely to a composite digital printer. Colours will be reproduced to varying degrees of accuracy however they are specified.

Because most programs allow you both to change a colour's space and deliver it as either spot or process and to alter a colour without changing its name, it can be a bit confusing to the beginner.

For instance, Pantone 265 could be selected as a colour and specified as spot. Its space can be changed from Pantone to CMYK, whilst retaining its full Pantone name. Its colour can then be modified by altering the strengths of its constituent hues. Finally it can be changed to process. So here's a situation where a Pantone colour appears incorrect on-screen and separates out into CMYK values when printed.

Maintaining colour fidelity

Differences in colour space and device technologies can cause no end of problems unless a colour management system is followed.

These differences are caused by the varying colour gamuts of the devices in the workflow coupled with the deviation from the standard performance of individual devices.

Colour Management Systems (CMS) seek to remedy the situation by providing consistency and predictability. These systems work by profiling the performance of each device against an agreed standard and managing their differences as images 'pass through' each device.

Lately both the ICC (International Colour Consortium) and the ICM (Image Colour Management) have established standards for such profiles and this is recognised by the leading manufacturers of desktop publishing devices.

How colour management works

The underlying technology that allows colour management to take place on the Macintosh system is called ColorSync 2. Windows uses either Kodak or Linotype equivalents although ColorSync for Windows may soon be available.

Colour Management Systems are used to calibrate individual devices and manage the colour space conversion of images. External devices, such as offset-litho printing presses, are pre-calibrated by the manufacturers of these programs and supplied as ready-made ICC/ICM profiles.

The steps that need to be taken for colour management are as follows:

1 obtain ICC/ICM profiles of external devices, such as for offset-litho printing presses
2 calibrate each device – scanner, monitor, digital printer – by profiling them
3 use the profiles when scanning, viewing and outputting images

Calibrating devices

Scanners are calibrated by scanning specially prepared colour swatches and comparing the results to ideal values in a digital image of the swatches supplied on disk. The two sets of data are assembled to complete a profile specific to each scanning device.

Monitors are calibrated by measuring screen output using a colorimeter or spectrophotometer and comparing the results to ideal values which should be emitted. The two sets of data are assembled to complete a profile specific to each monitor. If no colorimeter or spectrophotometer is available, monitor data is entered in dialog boxes based on the monitor's specification.

Digital printers and printing presses are calibrated by printing colour swatches on each device. These swatches are reproduced from a digital CMYK image of swatches of known values. The printed results are measured using a colorimeter or spectrophotometer and compared with the CMYK values in the original image. The two sets of data are assembled to complete a profile specific to each output device.

Using the profiles

When images are scanned, viewed and printed the profiles that you've created or obtained should be referred to in order to achieve and maintain colour accuracy and consistency.

When scanning to RGB assign a profile for both the scanner and the monitor. When converting to CMYK assign a further profile, this time for the output device. You may have more than one output device, in which case two CMYK versions are required. If you are scanning direct to CMYK, assign a profile for both scanner and printing device.

In the case of proofing devices these should emulate the final printing press, in which case the printing press profile should be used. In Europe it would be one of the Eurostandard profiles; in the USA and Australasia one of the SWOP (Standard Web Offset Publications) profiles.

Profiles are selected within scanning controls, monitor settings, and mode conversion programs provided they support the ICC management system; in the case of Photoshop, which has its own mode conversion facility, profiles are selected within the colour setting controls.

—————— Organising text ——————

Text sources and copy editing

Text sources

Text in DTP documents can come from any source: from the DTP operator, from a team member or from an outside writer. But whatever its source it can be keyed directly into DTP documents or imported from text files (sometimes called electronic typescripts).

If a hard copy (handwritten or typescript) is supplied, provided it is legible it can be turned into an editable text file using an Optical Character Recognition (OCR) program. This avoids the drudgery of having to type out all the text from scratch.

Copy editing

All text needs to be copy edited before it's ready for publication. Copy editing can be substantive or detailed or may just involve removing inconsistencies. Substantive editing aims to improve the overall coverage and presentation of a piece of writing whilst detailed editing is concerned with whether a writer's meanings are clear, without gaps and contradictions. Ensuring consistency involves auditing spelling, punctuation, numbering and other issues of style.

Checking process

Substantive and detailed copy editing is normally undertaken from hard copy printouts from text files. The exception is when text is generated directly within DTP documents, in which case the hard copy print-outs are taken from DTP files.

As a general rule it's always better to proof text from printouts as mistakes can easily be missed on-screen. Text must always be checked against printouts in any case, as these are usually considered the definitive version at each production phase. But if the text has been heavily edited it should also be checked against earlier printouts.

Alterations should be made to hard copies in ink using special proof correction marks and following publishers' guidelines on style. The proof correction marks are designed to leave no room for ambiguity and thus facilitate the editing process.

Once the alterations have been made the text files are altered to match.

Final proofreading is done once page layouts have been finalised. Again this process is usually undertaken from hard copies taken from a DTP file. Alterations are then made to the DTP files either by the operator or by the copy editor.

Preparing material on disk

DTP documents should be supplied as files on disk rather than as hard copy for a number of reasons:

- the accuracy of the text is maintained, so proofreading is easier for both author and publisher
- it's possible to produce documents more quickly
- it's more cost effective

Text formatting

Ideally text should have the minimum of formatting:

- it should be left aligned
- it should not be indented
- words should not be underlined
- it should be untabbed where possible
- headings should not be capitalised
- a single typeface should be used
- a single font size should be used
- single spaces should be inserted between words and after punctuation
- two carriage returns to be inserted between elements (paragraphs, headings, etc.)

Saving files

- text files should be saved in an appropriate file format or as ASCII files
- each chapter or article should be saved as a separate file; very long chapters and articles should be split into smaller files.
- two copies of files should be supplied on disk and one up-to-date hard copy supplied on paper; paper copies are considered definitive versions if they vary from files
- paper copies should be annotated with appropriate file names and dates
- a copy of the final version of text should be kept on disk and paper
- the designer should be advised of any special characters used in the text, such as Wingdings fonts

Clearing text

If an extract is to be included it should be reproduced exactly as it appears in the original work. It's important to identify the copyright holder and obtain permission to use the piece.

In line with an agreement between the Society of Authors and the Publishers Association, extracts not exceeding certain limits may be quoted without permission, provided that acknowledgement to the title and author (not the publisher) is made where the extract appears in a document.

However, this 'fair dealing' agreement is not contained within copyright law and use of extracts may be challenged by copyright holders.

The following limits apply:

- 400 words (as one extract) from a book
- 800 words (as various extracts) from a book, provided no individual extract exceeds 300 words
- less than one third of an article from a newspaper, journal or magazine
- less than half of a poem

The following material is not covered by fair dealing:

- song lyrics or music
- material to be used in anthologies
- material which has been adapted in any way from the original
- where the extract is complete in itself (e.g. an article of 350 words)

Preparing indexes and glossaries

Compiling entries and forming indexes

You can begin by compiling your index as you write, either manually or using a word processor.

Go through the typescript selecting key words or phrases. Enter those on cards, noting typescript page numbers, then assemble the cards in alphabetical order. Convert the typescript page number to the document page number once the document pages are proofed.

Fig. 4.47 Index palette in QuarkXPress

Alternatively, select the entries as before but retain the cards in typescript page order until the document proofs are ready. Then enter the document page numbers in alphabetical order as you go.

Index entries may be single words, groups of words or whole topics. You should try to order long entries for ease of reference. For example, 'development of bridges' would be better arranged as 'bridges, development of' (Fig. 4.48).

If index entries are compiled manually in the manner described, advanced indexing techniques, such as Boolean operations and wildcard, can be employed if an index is automatically generated within page layout programs.

In some programs index entries can be made in situ. Text is tagged locally as an index [entry] and assigned one of several index levels. Tagging text this way is quite time consuming as all instances of a word need to be tagged to enable all the page numbers to be generated.

Big-end bearings:	street patterns, 338; ideal type of,
renewing, 25	*338*
sheel type, 33	structural determinism, 12
brake drum distortion, 58	Structure of this book, 27
Brake shoes:	*Studio International* (glossy maga-
cleaning, 56	zine), 52–53
Hobolt University, 125–345	Cassette recorder 88
architecture, 160	CD-player 90
faculties: Engineering, 276;	Citrus press 243
Science, 297; Art, 302;	Clock 65
Computer Science, 326	Cosmetic set 205

Fig. 4.48 Examples of index formatting: (top left) two-level, nested; (bottom left) two-level, nested with run-in; (top right) two-level, run-in; (bottom right) one-level

Cross referencing between index entries should be kept to a minimum and alternative entries, such as 'powered diggers' and 'diggers, powered' should be avoided.

Generating index entries and indexes automatically

Index entries can be compiled automatically within some programs on the basis of word frequency or from proper nouns.

Compiling entries on word frequency is fairly effortless but the resulting list often requires severe pruning. Compiling entries which are restricted to proper nouns is relatively easy but only useful for certain types of documents.

All four methods – manual, in situ, word frequency and proper nouns – can be mixed and matched to produce a final index using an indexing program. Probably the word frequency method is the most time consuming as the process of generation requires the elimination of words set in the wrong context.

Glossaries

Glossaries are an essential feature for documents which contain many technical words. Ideally the first or only occurrence of a technical term should be explained where it occurs in text. If a term is used more than once it is a candidate for inclusion in a glossary.

Glossaries can be prepared in much the same way as manually prepared indexes and should be compiled as you write. Key words to be included in a glossary can be highlighted with the text each time they appear. This way they can be easily checked against a printout of a glossary text.

As regards formatting, the first lines of glossary entries are usually set out as hanging indents so that referral is made easy.

Hierarchy of information

Text should be structured within text files on a hierarchical basis with each element – heading, text, caption, etc. – typed as a discrete paragraph unit.

Subheads should be limited to a maximum of three levels because of the difficulty of stylistically differentiating any number greater than this.

In cases where the levels are unclear, special codes could be inserted before paragraphs to indicate which level they are, e.g. chapter titles could be coded <CT>, first-level text headings <A>, illustration captions <ILC> and so on.

On-screen editing

Keeping backups

It's wise to keep historic backups of documents, in case of changes of mind. If you need to revert to an earlier version of the text, you simply open a backup file and copy across text to the current version.

Design and copy-led editing

Editing work is design, copy-led or a balance of both, i.e. text is edited so as not to compromise the design of a document, or its literary content or it is edited to meet a midway position.

Design-led editing is the most editorially challenging as copy lengths cannot be altered much, if at all, without compromising the design.

Showing 'invisibles'

You will find it easier to edit and enter text accurately with the invisibles showing (the symbols which represent non-printing characters, such as spaces or returns).

Editing order

The order in which you edit material can speed up your work. If you edit from back to front, i.e. starting at the end of an article and working towards the front, then you can edit text in the same place as your printout. If you work from the front, text reflows and the following text will be harder to locate.

Cutting, copying and pasting

Because paragraphs are a fundamental styling unit, it's important to avoid deleting ¶ marks in error as one of the merged paragraphs will take on the formatting of the other even when separated. This can easily happen when you are moving paragraphs around. To avoid such problems always highlight whole paragraphs, including the last ¶ mark and move the insertion mark in front of a paragraph before pasting. This way paragraphs maintain their integrity and thus their formatting.

'Dragging and dropping' text is a useful alternative to using menu commands or keystrokes but should be avoided during final editing as it's far too easy to move text around in error.

Entering text, returns and spaces

- there is no need to use a return at the end of each line – text will automatically wrap when it reaches the right edge of a text block or box
- type in upper and lower case at all times and apply capitals using the CAPS typestyle
- press Return when starting a new paragraph
- press Shift-Return to control line breaks within such text as a heading, address or verse

Special spaces

- press the spacebar to enter spaces between words
- use non-breaking spaces when you wish words to stay together on lines
- use fixed spaces when you wish spaces to retain their width in justified text
- use thin spaces where standard-width spaces are too wide but the removal of spaces gives too tight a setting

Applying text attributes

When you alter text attributes locally within programs such as QuarkXPress a plus sign appears beside the style sheet name in the Styles palette. This is quite normal as it indicates that further additional formatting is in force.

However, on occasions you may wish to remove any local formatting and return the text to its original formatting (to how the text looked before you made any changes). In most programs you choose No Style and then re-assign the style sheet; No Style breaks the link between paragraph and style sheet and when the style sheet is chosen, the full formatting is applied.

Copyfitting

This term describes the discipline of calculating text lengths in documents, taking into account column widths, font sizes and leading. Before DTP special tables were supplied by type foundries to assist in calculations. Nowadays, it's often easier to prototype columns of text on-screen and use the word counting facilities within programs.

Word or character counts – the average word length in non-technical English is six characters (including a space) – can be worked out for lines, column centimetres and/or full columns and should take into account paragraph spaces, subheadings, etc.

Keeping subheads with paragraphs

Ideally headings in text should remain with the paragraphs to which they refer. Otherwise you can spend a great deal of time reuniting paragraphs. You can set up your paragraph formats to do this automatically.

Removing orphans

Orphans, short lines isolated at the tops of columns, can automatically be avoided using the Keep Lines Together function within paragraph formatting controls.

Removing widows

Widows, short lines at the ends of paragraphs, should be removed locally by editing, by negative tracking (applied to the whole paragraph and not exceeding –4) or by applying a justification setting with a low minimum word spacing value of say 65 per cent.

Entering listings text

If you are entering listings text and its formatting changes from paragraph to paragraph, you can use the Next Style sheet command in some programs. This feature automatically rotates through a set of style sheets as you type.

Example:

Style 1	Next Style 2	**Manufacturer**¶
Style 2	*Next Style 3*	*Type of business*¶
Style 3	Next Style 1	Information…¶
Style 1	Next Style 2	**Manufacturer**¶

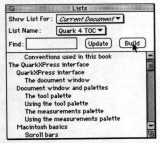

Fig. 4.49 Table of contents list in QuarkXPress

Table of contents

Table of contents can be automatically generated within some programs. A most efficient and reliable system is used by QuarkXPress (Fig. 4.49).

In QuarkXPress, style sheets for headings are effectively tagged for inclusion in a table of contents. The tags themselves are assigned their own style sheets so that when a table of contents is generated the text is correctly formatted.

Custom dictionaries

Custom or auxiliary dictionaries can be set up in some programs to enable you to spell-check words not included in standard dictionaries. Hyphenated words usually need to be entered as separate words. Some programs enable you to use dictionaries to control the automatic hyphenation of new words or to alter the hyphenation of those existing in the dictionary.

Points of style

Text areas with a clean, even texture (called colour), with thoughtful punctuation and simple formatting not only look good but enhance readability and ensure good communication. So, when detailing and formatting text aim for simplicity and clarity at all times.

Many large organisations publish authors' notes on grammar and text detailing, covering such areas as spelling, punctuation, numbering. If such house styles apply to the work you are doing adhere to their recommendations as closely as you can.

If no notes exist the following points of style may be of assistance to you. They are, however, intended only as an introduction to the sort of rules included in authors' notes and copy-editing handbooks and do not in any way aim to be either comprehensive or suitable for all types of documents. Refer to them only in the absence of any other suitable guidelines.

Abbreviations and contractions

Use the full point sparingly. Its main function is to denote the end of sentences. Only use a full point in other situations if its absence creates ambiguity (Fig. 4.52).

Most abbreviations are unambiguous without a full point and the following do not require punctuation:

- contractions: Mr, Mrs, Dr, St, Ltd
- common abbreviations: Esq, Rev, Co, Inc, mm, cm, km, kg, ms, ibid, per cent

---

The Very Rev Dr M C Mayo THEO DSO
requests the pleasure of...

Fig. 4.50 An example of the omission of full points in initials and an abbreviation

- units of measurement: ft, yd, yds, cwt, oz, lb, mph, kph
- groups of initials: BP, MIT, NEC, UK, UNICEF
- honours and awards: MA, PhD, FRIBA, MIEFE, DSO, CH
- post/zip codes
- BC, AD
- either p 57, pp 30–45, vol 18, fig 625, p21, no 5 with no full points but with a half word space before figures (in QuarkXPress flex space set at 25% per cent) or p.63, pp.80–95, vol.89, fig.204, pl.4 3, no.6 with a full point but no space after
- either *c*1900, *fh*1800, *d*1643 in italic with no full point and no space after. Or: use *c.*1900, *fl.*1800, *d.*1643 in italics with a full point and no space after
- format 6 am, 11.30 pm with half word space after figures and no full points either within or following am, pm
- omit after initials before a surname and use normal word spacing: J C Bull, John C Bull. If you use full points, follow them by a half word space (in QuarkXPress flex space set at 25 per cent): J.C.Bull, John C.Bull. Never omit spaces between initials
- ranks: Lt Col, Maj Gen, Capt or, preferably, spell in full
- Rt Hon, MP.
- format 95 kg with half word space after figures and no full points
- use an ellipsis... (not full points...) as a tail off
- use '&' only in names
- include after no. (number)

The word inch should be spelt out within sentences. In catalogue entries (especially if preceded or followed by metric equivalents) it may be abbreviated to 'in' without a full point. Spell out Professor (not Prof.)

Commas

Omit commas after street numbers and between the name of a city/town and the postal code.

Omit in dates: 3 March 1999.

Omit between a name and the honour/award, and between awards: C Hodder MA.

In science and maths books omit commas in figures in thousands (5673) and add a word space to five or more digits, except in tables where both occur, in which case four figure numbers should be spaced too: 56 234, 5 673.

In general books, use commas in figures in thousands: 5,673, 56,234.

Capitals, small capitals and non-aligning figures

If the font includes them use non-aligning figures in preference to aligning figures, except within tables, unless a traditional look is preferred.

Use small capitals for groups of initials, postal codes (when non-aligning figures are used), complete words or phrases in capitals within the text, and so on.

Avoid using capitals reduced in size within continuous text, as they will appear too light in relation to the lower-case letters.

Use small capitals for groups of initials consisting of more than three letters.

Countries should always be in full capitals: UK, USA.

If a group of initials is followed by a word commencing with a capital, this group is best in capitals: ICI Chemicals, not ICI Chemicals.

Format Roman numerals mostly in small capitals with capitals used only to give necessary weight.

Use capitals up to V, small capitals thereafter: vol IV, vols xviii–xxii.

Use capitals for kings and queens: Elizabeth I, Henry VIII.

Format MS, MSS in small capitals with no full points.

Use small capitals, with lower case where necessary, for honours and awards: BSC, PhD.

Use small capitals for BC, AD except with aligning figures.

Use small capitals for quoted words originally in capitals.

Numbers and figures

Use from 500 to 600 or 500–600, not from 500–600. Use an en dash with no spaces, not a hyphen.

Reduce the space before the number 1 in normal text (kern to the left of the 1 by approximately –0.2 en).

Dates should be given as 1808–9, 1808–12, 1820–21. Use an en dash with no spaces. Do not repeat the century: 1780–1820, 1720–30, not 1720–1730.

Set 28 July 1946, in that order, with no commas, no th, st, nd or rd; 1960s, not 1960's; 28 July–8 Aug, not 28–8 Aug; 250 BC, but AD 250; use oblique stroke for parts of the calendar year: 1999/2000.

Set 18 ft, 21 mm with a half word space.

$$28\times36\times54 \text{ mm}$$
$$28\times36\times54 \text{ mm}$$
$$28 \times 36 \times 54 \text{ mm}$$

Fig. 4.51 Examples of setting dimensions without spaces, with half-word spaces and with word spaces

Avoid starting a sentence with a figure.

Avoid II in lining figures.

Set twenty-one, for instance, with a hyphen.

Format 2.66 not 2·66, 0.45 *not* .45, 3 *not* 3.00.

Omit spaces in figure/letter combinations: 3c, 165s.

Set 210×297 mm, $8\times2\times48$ in; mm or in appear after the final dimension and should be preceded by a half word space (in QuarkXPress flex space set at 25 per cent). The × should be set in Symbol (Alt-Y), match the x-height of the accompanying text and have half word spaces either side. If the Symbol font is not available, use a lower case x, preferably from a sans serif font such as Helvetica (Fig. 4.51).

Italics

Use italics for:
- titles of printed works
- works of art
- names of ships, not types
- genera, species and varieties
- foreign phrases not commonly used in English texts
- directions to the reader
- emphasis, but sparingly

Use italic punctuation within italic phrases only, not before or after: In *What is Mathematics Really*, Hersh explores...

Use an italic colon after italic subheadings: *Areas of interest:*...

Hyphens and dashes

Use hyphens (-) in compound nouns and double-barrelled names and discretionary hyphens for line breaks. These hyphens automatically disappear if editing makes the hyphens redundant.

Use en dashes (–) not hyphens with word spaces either side as a substitute for colons and parentheses or to denote a duration.

Also use en dashes for compound adjectives when one of the items is made up of two words or a hyphenated word.

Use an en dash with a word space before to indicate an abrupt break in speech: "I told you –"

14.30–20.30
January–July
16–18 year olds
London Gatwick–Paris Orly flight

Fig. 4.52 The use of en dashes with and without half-word spaces

Use em dashes (—) with or without word spaces either side as an alternative to colons and parentheses or to indicate a change of thought.

Use em dashes to indicate the omission of a word in text or figure in a table: The Keeper of the Archives Mr C—considers...

Em dashes may also be used as a substitute for bullet points.

Then General Dashwood-Smithe began
singing – he often did when drunk...

Then General Dashwood-Smithe began
singing—he often did when drunk...

Fig. 4.53 The use of hyphens, en dashes and em dashes

Brackets
Use parentheses ( ) for brackets, except in quotations (see below)

Quotations
Either use single quotation marks but double quotation marks for quotations within quotations or double quotation marks but single quotation marks for quotations within quotations.

Use square brackets [ ] for text inserted in quotations when the insertion has been written by someone other than the original author.

'John said "Can't you come to the
theatre?" and I told him...'

Fig. 4.54 An example of the use of double quotation marks
within single quotation marks

Set long quotations in a smaller font size, without quotation marks, with a half line space before and after, with or without left and right indents. Alternatively, use the normal text size, with quotation marks, half line space before and after, and not indented. If the main text is justified, use left alignment without any indents.

Position full points and commas inside quotation marks. If the quotation is at the end of and part of a larger sentence, position the full point outside the quotation marks.

Position colons and semi-colons outside quotation marks.

Bullets and numbered lists
Use fixed width or en spaces between bullet/numbers and following text unless hanging indents are used.

Set (5) *not* 5) when set out from paragraph.

Numbering systems

Documents more than a few pages long need to be clearly page-numbered so that users can easily find their way around. Usually chapters, sections and pictures also need to be numbered for ease of reference.

This is especially true for documents designed specifically for reference purposes as their content needs to be easily and effectively retrieved by users. Otherwise information contained between their covers might never be accessed and used which would defeat the object of publishing such documents in the first place.

It's important therefore to have some knowledge of key numbering techniques before embarking on any multipage and multisectioned document.

As the application of the techniques themselves often helps to clarify content structure, their usefulness as both 'design tools' and 'signposting' devices is best appreciated if they are applied early on in a project rather than being added as an afterthought.

Page numbering systems

Simple documents are usually numbered from their first page to their last page using Arabic numerals. Invariably hard covers are not counted as pages although self-covered documents (documents whose covers are printed on the same type of sheets as their inner pages) may be counted in or out.

More complex documents may have preliminary pages (pages preceding their main content) and end matter such as appendices. These pages may be numbered separately from the main body of a document, e.g. prelims may be numbered in lowercase Roman numerals – i, ii, iii, iv, v... – with the rest of the document, including any index, numbered in Arabic numerals – 1, 2, 3, 4, 5...

Chapter and section numbers may be in either Arabic or Roman.

Pictures, figures and tables are usually numbered in Arabic numerals.

An alternative numbering approach is based on the Universal Decimal Classification system (UDC), originally developed for book classification in libraries throughout the English-speaking world.

It is particularly suited to multisectioned documents, especially documents of a technical nature, as it is logical and easy to follow.

It exploits the fact that decimal numbers can be added to after the decimal point without affecting the existing sequence. The sequence of numbers can take the reader to a specific page, i.e. 6.3.12 relates to the main section 6, subsection 3 (within this section), page 12 (within this subsection).

Before

1, 2, 3, 4, 5, 6, 7, 8, 9, 10, 11, 12, 13...

After

1, 2, 3, *4*, *5*, *6*, *7*, *8*, *9*, *10*, *11*, *12*, *13*, *14*, *15*...

Before

1.1, 1.2, 1.3, 1.4, 1.5... 2.1, 2.2, 2.3, 2.4, 2.5... 3.1, 3.2, 3.3, 3.4, 3.5...

After

1.1, 1.2, 1.3, 1.4, 1.5... 2.1, 2.2, 2.3, 2.4, *2.5*, *2.6*, *2.7*... 3.1, 3.2, 3.3, 3.4, 3.5...

Fig. 4.55 If additional pages are inserted into a document when using a normal numbering system, all pages following the insertion will need renumbering. Using a decimal system only following pages within a section are affected. White numerals indicate new pages; *italicised* numerals indicate renumbered pages

——————— 5 ———————

VOLUME PRINTING

This chapter covers:
- pre-press and printing
- papers and boards

——————— Pre-press and printing ———————

Before I proceed, I need to explain the terms 'pre-press' and 'printing'. Pre-press traditionally embraced all the processes involved between the artwork phase and final printing, and printing involved one or other or a mix of conventional processes, such as offset-litho and silkscreen.

Nowadays, as DTP artwork is digital and volume printing can either be digital or conventional, the pre-press phase is less distinct. Many digital technologies, such as imagesetters, have replaced traditional pre-press methods and these, in turn, in some cases are already being superseded by even newer technologies, some encroaching on the printing process itself.

Printing itself is undergoing a revolution, with digital and hybrid systems both taking work away from conventional presses and creating new markets for themselves.

Much of the development work is driven by the need to keep as much of the production process digitally on-line, i.e. to extend the

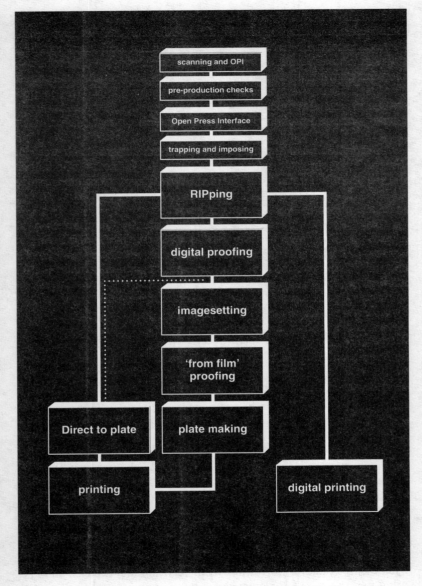

Fig. 5.1 The production workflow. Dotted lines indicate alternative flow

DTP process right into the printing presses themselves. It's also driven by the need to control workflow from the desktop. 'Print on demand' is a term used to describe such desktop control.

About two-thirds of printed documents around the world are created digitally using DTP technologies so it makes sense for printing to become part of the same regime.

Pre-press

The pre-press process embraces the scanning and import of images into documents, proofing work, imagesetting and platemaking.

Colour correction is an intrinsic part of scanning whilst basic retouching work is an optional add-on. Images are often imported into documents, either manually or by using Open Press Interface. OPI is a system of file substitution whereby production-resolution images are substituted for low-resolution counterparts during the imagesetting process.

For conventional printing DTP documents are rasterised and imageset. Bromides are usually output for line work, restricted to one or two colours, whilst film positives (and sometimes negatives) are output for any work involving halftones.

Before imagesetting multipage documents, their pages are reordered – 'imposed' – for the printing press. The imposition process takes into account printed sheet sizes, folding and binding methods and such aspects as page bleed and creep. Digital proofing often takes place prior to imagesetting for any document involving images and colour work.

From-film proofs are sometimes produced in addition to or instead of digital proofs so as to check the quality of film output, especially in respect of colour registration. Alternatively 'wet proofs' are produced once printing plates have been made.

Printing plates are mostly imaged from film output using photographic methods. Bromides are also used to image plates but more often films are produced from the bromides using reprographic cameras and these films are used for platemaking. Once the plates are imaged, they are ready for installing on a printing press.

One of the most recent developments in the area of pre-press is the introduction of computer-to-plate technologies (CTP). Digital files using this system are sent via a raster image processor (RIP) and imaged direct to metal printing plates, obviating the need for bromide or film.

Conventional printing

Traditional processes still dominate quality printing and will do so for some time. Most modern presses are extremely reliable, and being computer controlled they achieve high and consistent standards of quality currently unmatched by any digital methods.

Offset-litho is the mainstay of commercial printing although it does have its drawbacks. Very short runs are expensive in terms of cost per sheet. To address this weakness, one company, Heidelberg, has pioneered the use of digital systems within its offset presses. The resultant print quality is as good as that achieved using conventional methods and far superior to the output of digital presses produced by Xeikon and others. See later in this chapter.

Offset-lithography

Offset-litho accounts for nearly half of all conventional (non-digital) printing and gives very high-quality results at reasonable costs. It is available as sheet-fed (suitable for printing up to 75,000 copies) and web (suitable for printing 75,000 copies and above).

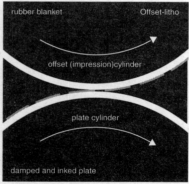

Fig. 5.2 Offset-litho printing process

The process. The planographic process exploits the well-known fact that water and grease don't mix. Thin metal plates are prepared with a greasy image using photographic methods. The plates are then secured to cylinders which are rotated. Whilst rotating, the plates are lightly damped and then inked. Since a film of water lies over all non-greasy areas, the printing ink adheres only to the image areas.

The ink is then transferred – 'offset'– onto smooth rubber-covered cylinders and from there onto sheets or rolls of paper (Fig. 5.2).

Flexography

Flexography accounts for around a quarter of all conventional printing as it's the mainstay of packaging production. Essentially it's a form of letterpress printing using rubber relief plates.

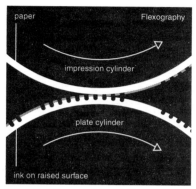

Fig. 5.3 Flexographic printing process

The process. Ink is rolled onto the raised surfaces of 'rubber' plates. Those portions of the plates which are not to print are below the inked surface. Halftone plates consist of a plateau of raised dots of varying sizes. Where the image is darker the dots run together, and portions which are not printing become isolated pits (Fig. 5.3).

In conventional letterpress, plates are made of metal and are either flat or curved; the latter are used on rotary presses for newspaper and magazine production.

Photogravure

Around a tenth of all printing is done by photogravure which gives very high-quality results. But because its setup costs are high, this method of printing is generally restricted to high-volume magazine production with runs, of say, 1,000,000 copies or more.

The process. The surface of gravure plates are pitted all over with small square recesses or cells of varying depth using photographic methods. Ink is rolled onto the surface of plates which are attached to rotating cylinders. The surfaces of the plates are wiped clean and the ink is drawn out onto absorbent paper pressed against its surface by another cylinder (Fig. 5.4).

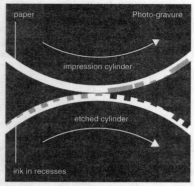

Fig. 5.4 Photogravure printing process

The deeper the recesses, the stronger the ink image. Theoretically it's the most subtle of the four processes described in this section, but a great deal depends on the paper quality used and the skill of operators and platemakers.

Silkscreen
Silkscreen is mostly used for point-of-sale and poster work, although the monopoly it has held in these areas is being eroded by digital methods.

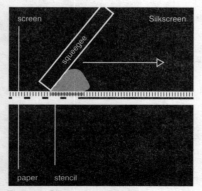

Fig. 5.5 Silkscreen printing

The process. A stretched printing screen (in the past screens were made of stretched silk) is coated with a sensitised solution and an image transferred onto it. Those parts of the screen which are not to print are chemically hardened. Ink is then squeezed through the open parts of the screen onto sheets of paper (Fig. 5.5).

Tonal images consist of a pattern of open dots. The larger the dots, the darker the tones, as in flexography and offset-litho printing.

Digital press and 'print on demand'

The terms digital press and print on demand are often misused when high-volume digital printing is discussed. The terms are not synonymous although many people use them interchangeably, implying that installing a digital press automatically gets you print on demand.

Digital press is any piece of high-speed printing equipment that creates multiple high-quality copies directly from an electronic file. The Canon Color Laser Printer, Xeikon DCP, Agfa Cromapress, IBM InfoCor 70, Xerox Docutech, IBM 3170, Scitex Spontane, Indigo E-Print 1000 and Heidelberg Quickmaster DI all fall into this category.

Print on demand is a process and suite of software that manages documents from the originator's workstation to the printing device and bindery.

The objective of both systems is to automate the printing of documents which are currently done off-line using offset-litho presses or xerographic (laser) printing devices. As around two-thirds of all printed documents are created using DTP technologies it makes sense that volume printing when appropriate should be included in the digital process.

Although digital laser printers have been around since 1985, they are mostly suited to printing a few copies of documents (apart from the Canon Colour Laser Printer and equivalent printers from Xerox and Kodak). It is only really now that the technology exists for producing documents in high volumes and at near-offset-litho quality.

Digital presses
Digital technologies are making in-roads into many print applications, particularly for documents requiring low quantities (between

50 and 5,000). However, as the technologies develop and their print quality improves, these presses could eventually supply all but the highest-volume and highest-specified print work.

Most of these presses combine image lasers or LEDs with new types of plates, drums and inks. Not only do the presses let you image documents directly on the presses themselves, but they also automate document management and make-ready, eliminating the time-consuming and costly preparation of film, plates and water-based inks.

Price per copy, up to 500 copies, is much less than that of conventional offset-litho. Because the presses are fully automated, they offer very fast turnarounds and some allow variable text changes (text changes between individual copies).

Apart from the Heidelberg Quickmaster DI, the presses at present can't match the quality of conventional offset-litho printing – nor are they able to print varnishes or metallic and fluorescent colours. Having said this, their quality is surprisingly good, perhaps midway between standard laser proofs and offset-litho prints.

Indigo E-Print process. A special rewritable plate is permanently secured to a cylinder which is rotated. Whilst rotating, image areas are charged by an array of lasers, taking data directly from a RIP (Raster Image Processor). Fine ink particles in liquid suspension and given an opposing charge are injected at the plate. The ink is then transferred – 'offset'– in a semi-solid state onto a smooth rubber-covered cylinder and from there bonded onto the paper. No ink residue is left on the offset cylinder and the precisely deposited particles are instantaneously bonded to the paper, enabling trimming and finishing work to be immediately carried out.

Benefits of Indigo E-Print system over other systems:

- variable text changes are possible
- colours are more brilliant and subtle than with the Xeikon system
- type and halftone dots are even sharper than conventional offset-litho (200 lpi screens are possible from 2,200 dpi machine dots)
- some models allow two spot colours in addition to CMYK
- can print automatically on both sides of a sheet
- available in sheet-fed and web form
- last-minute design changes are fast, easy and inexpensive to make

Xeikon process. Special rewritable plates are permanently secured to cylinders which are rotated. Whilst rotating, image areas are charged by an array of LEDs, taking data directly from a RIP. Fine particles of dry ink toner are given an opposing charge, adhering to the image areas on the plate. The ink is then transferred directly to the paper. The precisely deposited particles are heat-bonded to the paper enabling trimming and finishing work to be immediately carried out (Fig. 5.6).

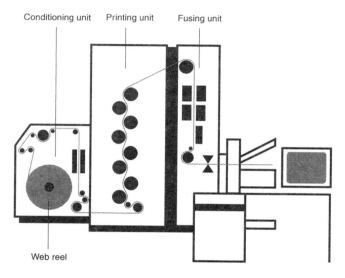

Fig. 5.6 The reel-fed Xeikon DCP digital press

Benefits of Xeikon system over other systems:

- variable text changes are possible
- both sides of a sheet are printed simultaneously
- last-minute design changes are fast, easy and inexpensive to make
- adhesive coated, polyester and transparent substrates can be printed on in addition to paper

Heidelberg Quickmaster DI process. This digital press is essentially an offset-litho press with a digital imaging mechanism substituting for the damping and inking systems. Specially treated silicon plates take the place of the litho plates. Whilst rotating, the plates are imaged by an array of laser beams taking data directly from a RIP. The beams etch small depressions into the silicon surface not unlike in the gravure process which I covered earlier. The plates are then inked with waterless ink. Since the silicon-covered areas repel the ink it is accepted only by the recessed image areas. The ink is then transferred onto smooth rubber-covered cylinders and from there onto sheets of paper in the same way as in conventional offset-litho. Because the plates can't be re-imaged, material for 35 plates is stored on cassettes within the main drum unit.

Benefits of the Quickmaster system over other digital systems:

- high ink density is possible because the SWOP inks are absorbed by the paper
- good registration, although trapping is still necessary
- various substrates can be printed on in addition to paper

Speciality printing

There are many special printing techniques available to enhance your printed communication. As most are craft based they are relatively costly and therefore more suited to documents of a prestigious nature.

The techniques can be used on their own or in conjunction with other printing processes, particularly with offset-litho.

Engraving

Engraving is perhaps one of the oldest printing techniques and one employed by artists no less than William Blake, Cruikshank and Dürer.

Once artists worked directly on the surface of a metal die or copper plate with a burin, the shadow and tonal areas being achieved by cross hatching. Nowadays photographic methods allow artwork to be created separately and its images used to stencil either copper or steel plates which is then engraved using chemicals.

The plates are printed using the intaglio method. Ink is forced into the crevices of plates and their surfaces are wiped clean. Damp sheets are pressed against the plates which suck ink out of the plates' crevices onto the paper surfaces.

The technique is now little used and mainly restricted to traditional-style letterheads and invitations.

Diestamping

Diestamping involves creating a steel die with the image recessed similar to gravure, but without its cell structure. Ink is rolled on thickly and non-printing areas are cleaned off by a wiping action against a roll of kraft paper. To produce maximum effect and ink transfer, card is glued to the impression surface. This is so cut that the paper being printed is embossed, thus raising the surface where there is printing. The result is a printed image of considerable relief with the surface looking enamel-like.

The technique works well on both printed and unprinted areas but is not suitable for laminated, varnished or cast coated materials. It is mainly used for high-quality letterheads and promotional work.

Blind embossing

Blind embossing is a similar process to diestamping but does not print the upper surface of a sheet. Its effect is understated in comparison unless used in conjunction with foil blocking. As with diestamping it's not suitable for laminated, varnished or cast coated materials.

The technique is mainly used for high-quality stationery and promotional work.

Thermography

Thermography creates a similar effect to diestamping without involving costly steel dies. The process begins as offset-litho or letterpress. Powdered resin is sprinkled onto the wet ink and fused to the sheet through the application of heat to give a rich, glossy raised surface. The finished result tends to be a bit 'orange-peely' so the technique is best restricted to less prestigious items, such as greetings cards and wrapping papers.

It works well on both printed and unprinted areas but like diestamping it's not suitable for laminated, varnished or cast coated materials.

Hot foil blocking

Hot foil blocking is a modern variant of an age-old process of applying precious metals in leaf form to book covers and pages.

Today glossy metallic coloured foils are used instead of hammered metals and the material is laid down by the pressure of a heated die instead of by hand. Fine details and good registration can be achieved with this technique.

The process works well on most laminated and coated materials and can be followed up by blind embossing to further enhance a design. It is mainly used for high-quality stationery items and promotional work.

Papers and boards

Many types of papers and boards are available to the desktop publisher including designer selections, packaging papers, security papers and commodity products. Whilst the majority are made from natural materials such as wood pulp, some are synthetic, being manufactured from polymers and other complex chemical constituents.

The range of recycled products – products made wholly or partly from recycled stock – is now quite wide and provides a viable alternative to conventional substrates for the environmentally-conscious.

Recently specially approved papers have been introduced to meet the needs of digital presses and special solutions developed to treat conventional stock so that they can be used successfully on such presses.

Coated and uncoated papers

The papers and boards used for most desktop publishing work fall within two broad categories: coated and uncoated.

Coated stock has a smooth surface which can be matt, silk, satin or high gloss in finish. The low-reflectivity and subtle appearance of matt and silk/satin finishes make them a firm favourite amongst most designers. To some, however, only a glossy surface speaks of quality.

Coatings applied off-machine are of higher quality than machine coated, whilst cast coated gives the glossiest finish.

Uncoated stock is invariably rough as it lacks the clay coating that evens out the surface bumps of coated stock. But the absence of a coating means the paper is partially absorbent and therefore suitable for documents which need to be written on. Banks, bonds, carbonless copying papers, cartridge papers and some boards fall into this category, making them eminently suitable for a wide range of stationery and business literature.

Specialist products

Specialist products include one-sided boards (boards coated on one side only), label papers (for packaging and other applications), embossed papers and boards, security products (for coupons, share certificates, etc.) and kraft, glassine and vegetable parchment (for packaging work).

Synthetic products

There are many synthetic materials on the market, ranging from aluminium-finished label products through to tear-free packaging papers. Some have been developed purely for creative effect whilst others are strictly functional. Dupont's Tyvek, made from spun-bonded olefin, is an example of the latter type. It was designed originally for mail enclosures but it's so strong that even disposable parachutes are made out of it.

Recycled products

Virtually any type of paper and board nowadays can be recycled and an elaborate system of grading and sorting ensures that the maximum value is obtained from recovered fibre.

Since waste fibre is weaker than new fibre and generally contaminated, this limits the range of recycled products available to the desktop publisher. Having said this, most paper and boards contain a proportion of recycled content, however small.

Fig. 5.7 USA and Canada's
Mobius Loop device used to indicate
that a product is recyclable

Identifying products with a genuinely high content of recycled fibre is not always easy despite the proliferation of environmental labelling.

Here are just some of the labels currently in use today: Germany's Blue Angel, Green Dot and ReSy, the Nordic White

Swan, Sweden's Good Green Buy, Canada's Environmental Choice, the Austrian Eco-label, the European Community (EC) Eco Label, UK's REPAK, BSi Standard and National Association of Paper Merchants (NAPM) Recycled Paper Mark, USA and Canada's Mobius Loop which comes in two versions: one denoting that a product is recyclable (Fig. 5.7), the other denoting that it is made entirely from, or contains, a percentage of recycled fibre.

Digital press products

Most paper and board products are designed for conventional printing processes and as a result sometimes they don't run well, if at all, on digital presses. Only a few are designed specifically for the purpose.

Papermakers Enso were the first to launch a special digital range approved for Agfa, Xeikon, IBM and Indigo presses. However there's some debate as to the type of paper best suited to digital printers. Certainly colour photocopiers, inkjet printers/proofers and Xeikon and Indigo presses provide better copies with smoother surface finishes. Xeikon claims that it doesn't matter whether surfaces are rough or smooth, and that most papers run on its presses with equal quality.

Indigo's E-Print is effectively an offset press and as such it should be tolerant to uncoated surfaces; in practice, however, it has shown to be more suited to smooth-coated stocks. This does not mean that printing stationery items on uncoated stock isn't possible, or even difficult, provided they are treated with a special water-based solution supplied by Indigo.

It will soon be possible to print on almost any substrate with Indigo's E-Print, with polyester and plastics already an option. This is just as well, as synthetic papers are becoming more popular.

Indigo recommend weights from 115 and 270 g/m^2, although weights as low as 80 g/m^2 and as high as 400 g/m^2 can be used.

Xeikon and its partners Agfa and IBM have appointed The Rochester Institute of Technology in New York to provide centralised substrate testing and evaluation facilities. Its CIMSPrint Digital Printing Laboratory is responsible for supplying accreditation details and associated optimum press operating parameters for Xeikon engine distributors and operators. It offers its specialist services to paper manufacturers and merchants seeking official digital print certification.

Weights as low as 60 g/m² and as high as 250 g/m² can be used on Xeikon presses. Certified products from Robert Horne in the UK include Royal Digital Gloss and Silk (from 115 and 200 g/m²), Neusiedler Color Copy-R (from 90 and 250 g/m²) and Raflatac Digi Cast and Digi Vellum self adhesive papers (in 83 g/m² only).

Weight ranges

The weight of paper is measured in grams per square inch. Banks are generally from 40 g/m² and 60 g/m², bonds 70 g/m² and 170 g/m² and cartridge 115 g/m² and 170 g/m². Board weights are usually from 200 g/m² and 300 g/m² but sometimes they are described in terms of their caliper (their thickness in microns (μm)), the equivalent being 180 to 285 μm.

Optical and surface characteristics

Here are some optical and surface characteristics which need to be taken into consideration when selecting a paper/board stock:

- hue – the spectral colour; pink, yellow, green, blue etc.
- saturation – in this context the shade of a hue, from deep to pale
- brightness – in coated stock, this property is very much dependent on the brightness of the underlying substrate
- fastness to light – the degree a sheet discolours over time
- opacity – the extent a sheet is impervious to show through. This property is closely related to the bulk of a paper; small changes in thickness can significantly alter a paper's opacity
- finish – the degree of smoothness of the surface texture as felt by the fingers and seen by the eye, ranging from super-calendered (ultra smooth and glossy) to highly embossed (heavily undulating)

GLOSSARY

Adobe Type 1 fonts PostScript technology used by font manufacturers

alert box dialog box on a screen alerting you to the consequences of a decision you are about to make

anti Alias addition of pixels with intermediate values along edges to reduce the 'staircasing' effect of a bitmapped representation

ASCII American Standard Code for Information Interchange; standard format for representing digital information in 8-bit chunks

baseline imaginary line on which upper and lower case letters sit; descenders extend below this line

Bézier curve mathematically defined curve used in graphics programs

binary the base-2 numbering system that most computers use

bit binary digit; smallest possible unit of information that a computer can process

bit depth a measure of the amount of information recorded or displayed for each pixel

bilevel 1-bit image. *See* bitmap

bitmap representation of characters or image by individual pixels (or dots); 1-bit image. *See* bilevel

bitmapped image image made up of pixels (or dots)

bleed extra amount of image extending beyond the trimmed edge of a page

brightness amount of white or black in a colour

bromide photographic paper used by imagesetters for outputting camera-ready artwork

body non-printing height of a font

bureau company specialising in printing and/or imagesetting DTP documents (in this book, bureau refers also to a repro department at a printing works and a colour copy shop)

byte common unit of computer storage; a byte is 8 bits

cast overall colour bias

CCD charge-coupled device: a light-sensitive chip-mounted device used in scanners to convert light into an electrical charge

CD compact disk, a standard medium for storing digital data

character generic name for a letter, number, symbol or 'invisible'

check box small box that works as a toggle for selecting an option (when you click on an empty box an X or tick appears, turning it on; when you click again, the X or tick disappears and the option is turned off)

chooser Macintosh desk accessory used to log into devices such as printers and other computers linked to a network; also used to enable and disable AppleTalk, Apple's native networking protocol

clipboard area of a Macintosh's memory that holds what you last cut or copied; paste inserts a copy of the current contents of the clipboard

clipping path a vectored path which masks areas of an image when printed

CLUT colour look-up table; a colour-indexing system used by computers to reference colours if their systems don't support the correct bit-depth to represent all colours

CMYK cyan, magenta, yellow and key (black), the colour model used in the graphic and printing fields

colour separation process of separating colour originals into primary printing colours

column principal text and image areas, within the page margins

contone continuous tone: a photographic print, negative or transparency containing continuous tones

contrast the relationship between the lightest and darkest areas in an image

copyfitting calculation of how much space a given amount of text will take up at a given type specification; editing or formatting text to fit within prescribed text areas

cursor Latin word sometimes used to describe the pointer or the insertion point

cutout non-rectangular image

dialog box box on a screen requesting information or a decision from you

dot gain printing defect in which halftone dots print larger than they should be

dpi dots per inch: measurement of the density of information in an image; also the measurement of the resolution of printers and imagesetters. *See* ppi

DTP desktop publishing

drive floppy, removable or hard disk

drop cap large capital letter integrated within the first few lines of a paragraph

duotone two-colour halftone reproduction from a single grayscale image

em measure equal to the width of the square of a font size, e.g. a 15 pt en is 15 pt; used as a horizontal unit of measure. *See* en

en measure equal to half the width of the square of a font size, e.g. a 15 pt en is 7.5 pt; used as a horizontal unit of measure. *See* em

Ethernet industry standard networking and communications system using co-axial cable

field an area in a dialog box or palette in which you enter values

film photographic film used by imagesetters for colour separations

fixed space word space which doesn't vary in justified alignments

flex space user-definable space which doesn't vary in justified alignments

fold crease dividing document pages, not to be confused with a bound spine

folder subdivision (subdirectory) of a disk

font typeface comprising a collection of letters, numbers, punctuation marks and symbols with an identifiable and consistent appearance

format way of saving files and transferring data

foundry company which commissions, designs, makes and markets fonts

frame border around a text or picture box; a box rule

gamma measure of how compressed or expanded dark or light tones become in an image

gamut range of colours available in a particular colour system space (or mode)

grabber hand tool which allows you to move around a document without using the scroll bars

grayscale depiction of grey tones between black and white; usually composed of 256 greys

greek depiction of pictures and text as blocks of grey to speed screen redraw

grid network of column, margin and ruler guides which define the major alignments and principal spaces on a page

gutter vertical space between columns

halftone pattern (or screen) of dots of different sizes used to simulate a continuous tone photograph, either in colour or monochrome; measured in lines per inch

hard copy material in typed form

H&J hyphenation and justification: a function which controls the automatic hyphenation and justification of text within paragraphs

hue the colour component of colour, such as red or green

hyphenation breaking of words into two parts to improve word spacing

I Beam pointer's shape when dealing with text

image graphic, photograph or illustration

imagesetter digital phototypesetting machine capable of producing graphic images as well as type on bromide or film. (Most imagesetters are PostScript-compatible)

indent setback of lines of text within a paragraph

insertion point blinking vertical line indicating where the next keystroke will add or delete text

interpolation estimation of values between two known values; assignment of an intermediate colour to pixel based on the colour of the surrounding pixels

invisibles characters that don't print, such as [Tab] and [Shift]

item an element within a vectored document, such as a path or box

justification alignment of text at both sides of a paragraph through the adjustment of word spacing

KB kilobyte; a unit of measure equalling 1,000 bytes

kerning intercharacter spacing

keypad numeric keys on the right of the keyboard

keystrokes use of modifier keys with other keys to execute a command

leading distance between lines of text, usually measured between baselines

line printed rule; images which contain black and white areas, without intervening greys

line screen resolution of a halftone

lpi lines per inch: the measurement of a halftone screen

margin outer area of the page surrounding the principal text and image areas

master page page which provides document pages with their column and margin guides

master page items items on document pages provided by master pages

MB   megabyte: a unit of measure equalling 1,024 kilobytes

menu   list of commands

modifier keys   keys which modify the effect of a character key: standard modifier keys are [⌘], [Alt], [Shift], [Control] and [Caps Lock]

moiré   undesirable optical effect caused by overlaying dot patterns which are incompatible

monochrome   tonal original, in shades of only one colour, such as black

montage   collage of images

negative   image in which tone values are reversed – white for black, lights for darks

offset-litho   short for offset-lithography; the primary printing technology used in the printing industry

OPI   Open Press Interface: a system of file substitution

original   artwork or photograph which might be scanned

orthogonal   line which is either horizontal or vertical

page   one side of a leaf in a document

palette   small movable box containing commands

pasteboard   temporary storage and work area outside the page, the contents of which don't print out

PICT   Apple's native picture file format

pixel   picture element: the smallest distinct unit of a bitmapped image

plug-in   program which extends the functionality of Photoshop

PMS   Pantone Matching System: proprietary colour matching system used in the graphics and printing industries

point   unit of measure, approximately 0.353 mm

positive   image in which dark and light values are the same as the original; the reverse of negative

PostScript   Adobe's page description language used by QuarkXPress and other DTP programs

ppi   pixels per inch: measurement of the density of information in an image. *See* dpi

process colours   the CMYK colours used to reproduce colour photographs and illustrations

program   sequence of instructions that tell a computer what to do; also called software

progressives   proofs made from separate plates showing the sequence of printing and the result after each additional colour has been applied

printer digital desktop or commercial device for printing or proofing documents primarily using laser, inkjet, dye-sublimation or thermal wax technologies

QuickDraw programming routines that enable the Macintosh to display graphic elements on screen; also used to output text and images to certain non-PostScript printers; *See* PostScript

radio buttons group of small buttons for selecting an option, only one of which can be on at any one time

RAM random access memory: memory that a computer uses to store information it's processing at any given moment

rasterise conversion of page description information into a bitmap; the action of a RIP when attached to an output device

registration marks marks included on film separations for purposes of colour registration

remapping rearranging the dots within a bitmapped image

resampling adding, deleting or rearranging pixels within a bitmapped image

resolution in bitmapped images, the density of pixels; can also refer to their bit-depth

retouch removal of minor defects within an image

RGB red, green, blue; the colour model used by scanners and monitors

RIP raster image processor: part of a printer which converts page description information into a bitmap and sends it to the print mechanism

rivers unsightly gaps running vertically within text

runaround in QuarkXPress, the feature that controls the way text is displaced by boxes and images

running head header

scan bitmapped image created by scanner

scroll bars bars equipped with a scroll box and scroll arrows which enable you to scroll vertically or horizontally within windows

special colour *see* spot colour

spine binding edge of a document; part of a document's cover which is visible when placed on a shelf

spot colour colours other than the process colours printed as a separate colour within a offset-litho printed document; sometimes called special colour

style sheets stored grouping of text formats used to format paragraphs quickly and accurately

system fonts fonts which come standard with Macintosh and Windows systems

template document with special content that you use repeatedly to form the basis of new documents

TIFF tagged image file format, the defacto file format for saving scanned images

tiling printing document pages in sections

tracking word and letter spacing; used for copyfitting, styling and to improve readability

trapping technique use to minimise the effects of the misregistration of photo litho printing on a printed document

trim marks lines printed outside the edge of a document page for aligning guillotines

TrueType fonts Apple's own font technology used by the system fonts

TWAIN generic driver used to access scanning controls from within DTP programs

typography craft of designing with type

vectored drawing or object defined mathematically; sometimes called object orientated

vignette soft edge given to images

virtual memory a means of using storage memory on a disk to supplement RAM

window enclosed area on the screen in which a document appears

WP word processing

XTension third-party program which extends the functionality of QuarkXPress

INDEX

Adobe Type Manager 17
Adobe Type-1 17
alignment 80, 82
ANSI 102
Apple 12
ASCII 18, 102
baseline 63, 91, 93
binding methods 57, 159
bitmapped 14
blind embossing 167
bromides 159
bullet points 95
cameras 25
CMYK 15
ColorSync 16
colour palettes 15
columns 61, 63
computer-to-plate 159
CorelDRAW! 33
Cromalin 31
desktop 13
device-independance 17
dialog boxes 12
diestamping 167
digital press 54, 163
display 72, 78
draw 9
drop caps 95
dye-sublimation 19, 27, 29
emphasis 100
engraving 166

Ethernet 29
file formats 18
Flexography 161
folding methods 56, 159
font collections 37
forms 99
FreeHand 4, 33
from-film 29, 30, 159
graphical user interface 12
graphics tablets 27
grids 59
hot foil blocking 167
hypermedia 1
hyphenation 82, 85
Illustrator 4, 33
Image Colour Management 16
imposition 159
indents 95
inkjet 19, 27, 29, 30
International Colour
    Consortium 16
ISO 51
kerning 38, 102
laser 19, 27, 163
Laserwriter 3, 4, 19
leading 87
Macintosh 12, 22
margins 60
Matchprint 31
Microsoft 12
modular grids 63

monitor 23
Motorola 22
object-orientated 9
offset-litho 160, 163
Open Press Interface 159
Optical Character Recognition 42
page description languages 8, 17
page layout 7
page sizes 58
PageMaker 4, 31
Painter 4
Pantone 15
papers and boards 168
paragraph spacing 92
Pentium 22
photo-gravure 161
Photoshop 4
pixels 14
point 15
Portable Document Format 19
PostScript 3, 8, 19, 37
PowerPC 22
pre-press 157
print on demand 163

printing 157
proofers 29
QuarkXPress 4, 31
QuickDraw 19
QuickDraw GX 8
RAM 14, 22
RGB 15
sans serif 72, 77
scanners 24
script 72, 78
serif 72, 76
silkscreen 162
spacing text 82
symbol 72, 79
tables 97
thermal wax transfer 19, 27
thermography 167
trackballs 27
tracking 82, 89
TrueType 17
typography 71
variants 74
vector 9
Windows 12, 22
workflow 159
wysiwyg 4, 12, 14

Other related titles

HTML
PUBLISHING ON THE WORLD WIDE WEB
Mac Bride

If you are a World Wide Web user who wants to move on from browsing to publishing yourself then this is the guide for you.

HTML is the coding system used to create pages on the World Wide Web. With the aid of this book you will be able to create your own home page to tell the world about yourself or your business after only a few hours of practice. Once you have mastered the basics you can learn some of HTML's more advanced features such as making your page interactive or interlinked to other pages. At every stage, the essential principles will be explained and then demonstrated by a fully worked example.

Mac Bride takes the mystery out of the technical issues and jargon and provides an exceptionally clear introduction. The book assumes no previous knowledge and is suitable for the absolute beginner. It is ideal for anyone who wants to create their own home page on the Web whether for business or just for fun.

This edition has been updated to reflect the latest changes in the field of HTML publishing and page creation.

By the same author of *Teach Yourself The Internet*.

Other related titles

TEACH YOURSELF

THE INTERNET

Mac Bride

Travel the information superhighway with *Teach Yourself*!

The Internet is the global network of computing resources forming the much-talked-about information superhighway. On the Internet you can:

- send and receive electronic mail all over the world,
- get the latest news and information,
- chat to people through electronic newsgroups,
- go shopping,
- do business,
- play computer games,
- explore the World Wide Web, the vast world of hyperspace.

Mac Bride takes the mystery out of the technical issues and jargon and provides an exceptionally clear introduction. The book assumes no previous knowledge of computers and is suitable for the absolute beginner. It is ideal for anyone who wants to acquire a basic understanding of the Internet and would like to get on to it with the minimum of fuss and delays.

The book includes vouchers providing you with one month's free use of the Internet from two of the leading access providers.

'If you have been thinking about having a go on the Internet, but are worried it might be too technical for you, read this book first!' *Business Opportunity World*

Une heure plus tard

J'ai enfin réussi à réveiller Augustin.

Il a mis une bonne heure pour reprendre ses esprits. J'ai dû aller chercher de l'eau au puits pour lui mouiller la tête.

Augustin, réveillé, veut m'embrasser, il me dit qu'il est mon frère à la vie à la mort et se met à divaguer. Il me raconte, d'une voix pâteuse, une histoire sans queue ni tête.

Il a découvert un domaine mystérieux, il a été invité à une fête étrange. Les invités étaient en costume d'époque, il a rencontré une jeune fille très belle. La mariée n'est pas venue, alors le marié, qui s'est retrouvé seul, est parti...

endormir là. Il fait trop froid. Allons debout, marchez un peu... »

« Vacillant comme un homme ivre, le grand garçon, les mains dans ses poches, les épaules rentrées, s'en alla lentement sur le chemin de Sainte-Agathe... »

Il a le regard fixe, il parle comme un livre. Il s'interrompt parfois en affirmant qu'il n'est pas fou.

J'ai envie de lui dire : « Augustin, quand vas-tu atterrir ? »

Deux heures plus tard

Voyant qu'il reste dans les nuages, j'essaie de ne pas le contredire, je le laisse continuer.

Malgré l'envie que j'ai de rire, j'écoute avec le plus grand sérieux. Je fais semblant de m'intéresser, j'acquiesce tandis qu'il déraisonne, je lui pose même des questions, je lui demande les noms des personnages de sa fantasmagorie. Imperturbable, il me nomme Yvonne de Galais, Frantz de Galais. Des noms que je n'ai jamais entendus, qu'il a dû inventer.

Il veut retourner à la fête, retrouver les personnages de son délire. J'ai beaucoup de mal à le convaincre de me suivre à la maison.

Je lui fais remarquer que sa tenue laisse

à désirer, il a de la paille dans les cheveux, son vêtement est fripé. Plus grave, il a vomi sur son jabot.

Je promets de l'accompagner ensuite à la fête. Il accepte finalement de passer à la maison pour se changer.

Il exige d'emporter son petit fût.

L'après-midi

Notre mère l'accueille avec des larmes de joie, et bientôt de tristesse quand elle s'aperçoit qu'il pue l'alcool et surtout qu'il n'a plus sa tête. Augustin veut repartir à sa fête, puis tombe dans un état d'hébétude et s'endort profondément.

Maman en profite pour appeler le médecin.

Nous lui racontons tout ce qui s'est passé. Je rapporte mot pour mot les phrases d'Augustin. Le docteur hoche la tête, l'air soucieux.

« La situation est sérieuse, je vais l'examiner. » Notre mère le précède dans la chambre.

Augustin se réveille et accueille le médecin par un « Bonjour Princesse » très inquiétant.

Augustin se laisse ausculter avec bonne grâce, il s'adresse au docteur.

Il lui parle comme s'il s'agissait d'un tailleur en train de prendre ses mesures.

« N'oubliez pas que c'est un habit de cérémonie. C'est pour un mariage, je veux être le plus beau. »

Notre mère interroge le médecin.

« Il nous fait une crise aiguë de romantisme avec hallucinations. J'espère que c'est une folie toxique, compte tenu de la quantité d'alcool qu'il a absorbée.

— Que faut-il faire ? demande notre mère.

— Attendre. S'il s'agit d'une folie toxique, les symptômes devraient disparaître rapidement.

— Sinon ? demande ma mère, anxieuse.

— Si les hallucinations continuent, il va falloir le mettre à l'asile. »

Le docteur a prononcé le mot gravement et il a posé la main sur son épaule, en geste de réconfort.

Notre mère est livide, elle chancelle. Elle s'agrippe aux rideaux pour ne pas choir.

Augustin, son fils chéri, son poète, en camisole de force, au milieu des aliénés qui bavent. L'image est insupportable, c'en est trop.

Elle s'effondre en entraînant les rideaux. La lourde tringle de cuivre manque d'éborgner le docteur.

J'ai envie de rire, mais je crois que ce n'est pas le moment.

Dimanche 15 avril, 11 heures

Augustin s'est réveillé, il a réclamé un lait de poule, il semble redevenu normal. À notre mère qui lui apporte son lait de poule, il demande de lui chauffer un bain. Notre mère reprend espoir, elle pense qu'il a retrouvé sa tête.

Mais il ajoute : « Je dois être le plus beau de la noce, pour faire honneur à Yvonne. »

Maman s'effondre à nouveau. Elle maudit cette Yvonne qui lui a volé son fils, cette créature née d'un esprit dérangé et qui sans doute n'existe pas.

J'essaie de ramener Augustin à la raison. Brutalement, je lui dis : « Tu commences à nous courir, avec ton Yvonne. »

Lundi 16 avril

Le médecin a décidé un placement en asile. Maman, la mort dans l'âme, a dû signer le certificat d'internement.

Nous avons demandé à monsieur Fromentin de nous prêter sa carriole et sa jument pour conduire Augustin à l'asile de Vierzon.

Pour le persuader de nous accompagner, il a fallu une fois encore lui mentir. Nous lui avons dit que nous le conduisions à la noce.

Il a voulu alors mettre sa redingote et sa chemise à jabot de dentelle. Il a exigé aussi un bouquet de fleurs pour la mariée. Et il a voulu emporter son petit fût.

Le voyage a été très triste. La nature était à l'unisson. Le vent gémissait, les arbres noirs tendaient leurs bras décharnés vers le ciel gris, il tombait une sorte de neige fondue que le vent poussait sous la capote de la carriole. Nous étions trempés et glacés.

Maman pleurait, moi je n'étais pas très gai, je sentais que j'étais en train de perdre mon unique frère. Malgré tout ce qu'il m'avait fait subir, j'étais triste.

Seul Augustin avait l'air heureux, il croyait qu'il allait à la fête, il riait aux anges, il faisait des signes d'intelligence aux corbeaux, sa joie faisait mal.

L'arrivée à l'asile fut un moment pénible. Le préposé qui devait enregistrer l'entrée d'Augustin se révéla être un homme grossier. Il se moqua de lui, de sa redingote, et lui confisqua son petit fût. Tout à son rêve, Augustin ne se rendait compte de rien.

Dimanche 22 avril

Tous les dimanches, monsieur Fromentin nous conduit à Vierzon.

Nous passons la journée à l'asile. Le docteur est optimiste, il pense qu'Augustin est en train de guérir. Il est plus calme, il ne délire plus, il écrit beaucoup mais refuse de faire lire ce qu'il écrit. Il dit que ce sont ses secrets.

Il passe aussi son temps assis devant la fenêtre, à regarder le parc. Il semble y voir des choses étonnantes. Il frémit, prononce des mots inintelligibles. Il est comme le chat endormi qui rêve d'oiseau. Sans doute revoit-il des scènes de sa fête étrange, peut-être la fameuse Yvonne*.

---

* Qu'il prend d'ailleurs pour un oiseau page 77 du roman *Le Grand Meaulnes* : « *Elle était auprès de lui toute frémissante, comme une hirondelle un*

Il loge dans une chambre à deux lits. L'autre pensionnaire est un amnésique qui s'appelle Robert, il a perdu la mémoire après avoir reçu un cheval sur la tête. Il n'est ni méchant ni dangereux, il est doux, il joue aux dominos avec Augustin.

Robert ne se plaint pas de lui, sauf parfois la nuit. Quand Augustin se prend pour un cerf et qu'il brame.

instant posée à terre et qui déjà tremble du désir de reprendre son vol. »

Lundi 23 avril

Les longues soirées d'hiver sont longues. Surtout l'hiver.

Maman est triste, elle s'ennuie de son Augustin.

Ma présence lui est une maigre consolation. Je ne parle pas beaucoup, je n'ai pas grand-chose à lui raconter.

Quelquefois je parle du temps. S'il fait beau, je dis : « Il fait beau, espérons que ça va durer. » S'il ne fait pas beau : « Il ne fait pas beau, espérons que ça ne va pas durer. »

Et on en reste là.

Avec Augustin c'était différent, il avait toujours des choses à raconter, des choses étonnantes. Il y en avait tellement que ça lui est monté à la tête, et qu'il est devenu fou.

Moi je ne risque pas de devenir fou, il n'y a pas grand-chose dans ma tête mais au moins c'est bien rangé, pas comme dans celle d'Augustin.

Le médecin a dit qu'il faudrait faire le ménage dans cette tête. En profiter pour jeter tout ce qu'il y a d'inutile.

Dimanche 6 mai, matin

Augustin va mieux.

Le docteur lui a donné l'autorisation de venir passer un dimanche à la maison. C'est sa première sortie depuis qu'il est interné.

Nous avons été le chercher avec la carriole de monsieur Fromentin. Pendant le voyage, Augustin ne dit rien. Il n'a pas l'air content de revenir à la maison, il boude. Peut-être parce qu'on a refusé d'emmener son petit fût.

En traversant la forêt, monsieur Fromentin a dû s'arrêter pour laisser passer des biches. Augustin ne les a pas regardées.

Maman a préparé un repas de dimanche avec un poulet plein de blancs et tout ce qu'Augustin aime.

Elle a sorti de la cave une très vieille bouteille de vin, si vieille qu'on n'arrive plus à lire l'étiquette. Le docteur a interdit l'alcool pour Augustin, mais c'est dimanche et une petite goutte ça ne peut pas faire de mal. Augustin ne se contente pas d'une petite goutte. Sans que maman ose l'en empêcher, il vide la bouteille.

Comme il est sevré depuis un moment, l'effet de l'alcool ne se fait pas attendre. Il devient tout rouge, énervé, il parle beaucoup, il se met à bramer, il dit des bêtises et il chante des chansons pas jolies : « *Je suis ton cerf, cerf, cerf, serre-moi fort, et faisons des bichons, ma biche...* »

J'essaie de le faire taire par respect pour maman qui écoute, horrifiée.

Mais il continue, en pire. « *Avec Yvonne de Galais je vais me régaler, Galais, Galais...* » Tous les moyens que j'utilise pour le faire taire se révèlent vains.

Soudain je vois sur la desserte une grosse casserole en cuivre.

Je me revois bébé, j'imagine Augustin. Il brandit au-dessus de mon berceau une casserole avec laquelle il veut m'écraser la tête.

Augustin continue à chanter des horreurs.

Alors je me saisis de la casserole et sans réfléchir, comme poussé par une force secrète, je l'assomme.

Sa chanson « *Viens ma bique, que je te nique, que je te nique...* » cesse brutalement.

Maman, livide, se précipite sur Augustin estourbi et inconscient, elle s'écrie : « Tu as tué le Grand Meaulnes ! »

J'espère que ce n'est pas vrai, sinon je serais bien embêté.

Augustin n'est pas mort, au contraire. Le docteur qui l'a examiné le trouve beaucoup mieux.

Il s'est simplement interrogé sur la grosse bosse qu'il a sur le crâne. Par délicatesse, maman n'a pas osé dire que c'était son frère qui lui avait donné un coup de casserole sur la tête.

Le docteur, qui a parlé longuement avec Augustin, a remarqué une vraie amélioration de sa santé mentale. Il pense que, si les progrès se confirment, on pourra envisager une sortie définitive de l'asile.

Il faut croire que le coup de casserole lui a remis les idées en place. Si Augustin délire à nouveau, j'ai de quoi le calmer...

Dimanche 6 mai, le soir

Le retour à l'asile se passe beaucoup moins bien.

À un moment, nous croisons un troupeau de biches. Augustin se met à bramer désespérément, il appelle toutes les biches Yvonne et veut sauter par-dessus bord pour aller les rejoindre.

Monsieur Fromentin doit lâcher les rênes pour le maintenir sur son siège. Maman enfouit son visage dans son châle pour cacher ses larmes, moi je baisse la tête et mords mes lèvres, pour ne pas rire.

Mais le pire est à venir.

Tout commence avec des sonneries de cor qu'on perçoit au loin. Augustin manifeste d'abord une certaine inquiétude, il regarde la forêt avec un air de bête traquée, il se retourne sans cesse pour voir s'il n'est pas suivi. À un moment il s'assoit sous la banquette et enfouit sa tête entre ses genoux, comme s'il voulait se cacher. Son inquiétude grandit quand nous croisons l'équipage, les piqueurs, les sonneurs, les cavaliers.

Quand il voit la meute, il est pris d'une véritable panique. Il se lève de son siège, tout en sueur et pâle, puis, sans que nous puissions le prévoir, saute par-dessus bord de la carriole et s'enfuit au galop dans les fourrés.

Les chasseurs doivent retenir les chiens excités qui veulent le courser.

Monsieur Fromentin, qui avait lancé sa jument, a beaucoup de mal à l'arrêter. Cela lui prend un certain temps. Quand nous descendons, Augustin est loin.

Malgré l'aide que nous apportent les chasseurs et les chiens, Augustin reste introuvable. Le soir commence à tomber sur la forêt et les recherches doivent s'interrompre.

Augustin va passer la nuit dehors. Heureusement nous sommes au printemps, le temps est doux. Je ne suis pas trop inquiet pour lui. Augustin a déjà passé des nuits à la belle étoile et en plein hiver.

Notre mère, encore une fois désespérée, se tord les mains en évoquant les dangers de la forêt la nuit. Elle parle du Petit Chaperon rouge. Il faut appeler un médecin qui lui administre un calmant.

Lundi 7 mai

Pas de nouvelles.

Malgré des recherches confiées aux gen-darmes, Augustin reste introuvable.

La forêt garde son secret.

Notre mère dort encore, le calmant devait être très puissant.

Mardi 8 mai

Les gendarmes recueillent des témoi-gnages. Un braconnier prétend avoir vu dans la forêt un individu qui enlaçait une biche et l'embrassait sur les babines. Mais le braconnier était ivre.

Sa déposition a beaucoup choqué les gendarmes qui, pourtant, en ont entendu d'autres.

Mercredi 9 mai, le matin

Notre mère s'est enfin réveillée.

Heureusement, parce que tout le monde était un peu inquiet, même le médecin qui se demandait s'il n'y avait pas été un peu fort avec le calmant.

Elle veut savoir si on a retrouvé Augustin. Quand elle apprend que non, elle pousse un soupir et retombe en léthargie.

La nuit

Trois jours après la disparition d'Augustin, en pleine nuit, un chemineau hirsute se présente à l'asile de Vierzon, il n'est pas seul.

Il est accompagné d'une biche et de ses bichons.

Le gardien n'a pas voulu le faire rentrer, l'enceinte du bâtiment est interdite au gibier. L'individu a insisté pour voir le médecin chef.

Le gardien refuse, il ne peut pas réveiller le médecin à cette heure.

Le chemineau lui remet une lettre et disparaît dans la nuit avec son équipage.

Jeudi matin

Le médecin chef trouve sur son bureau la lettre.

Cher Docteur,

Pardon tout d'abord pour cette absence qui a dû vous inquiéter. Les lignes qui suivent vous fourniront, sinon une excuse, au moins une explication.

Après avoir sauté de la carriole, je me suis enfui dans la forêt. Me pensant poursuivi par les chiens, j'ai couru un moment. Les bruits ayant cessé, je me suis assuré que je n'étais plus suivi et j'ai erré dans la forêt.

Un bruit très faible, comme des sanglots, a attiré mon attention, il venait des épais fourrés. À pas de loup, je m'approchai et j'eus devant les yeux un bouleversant spectacle.

Au milieu d'une petite clairière, une biche pleurait, ses bichons émus et silencieux autour d'elle.

Dès qu'elle me vit, la biche, très digne

se redressa, sécha ses larmes et me souhaita la bienvenue. J'étais fort embarrassé, je ne voulais pas faire allusion aux larmes que je n'aurais pas dû voir, en même temps je souhaitais la consoler. Je me décidai pour une question neutre : « Puis-je faire quelque chose pour vous ? »

Elle me confia au milieu de sanglots qu'elle venait de perdre son mari. Son cerf chéri avait été abattu par de lâches chasseurs qui lui avaient tiré dans le dos. Elle me déclara qu'elle souhaitait en finir, rejoindre son cerf bien-aimé.

« Vous n'avez pas, par hasard, un glaive sur vous ? » me demanda-t-elle.

Puis, après un regard sur ses petits :

« Non je n'ai pas le droit, ils n'ont déjà plus de père », dit-elle.

J'eus de la peine à contenir mes larmes en regardant les bichons qui batifolaient, inconscients de la tragédie. J'étais très partagé, je voulais en même temps aller venger le cerf et aider cette mère courageuse.

Venger le cerf c'était affronter les chasseurs, cela était au-delà de mes forces. Je choisis d'aider la veuve. Je lui léchai ses larmes puis j'allai bichonner les bichons.

La biche, très maîtresse d'elle-même, me proposa avec simplicité des baies. Nous parlâmes de choses et d'autres, du goût des *feuilles, du temps, de l'éducation des enfaons**...

Au cours de la conversation, comme je l'appelais chère Madame, elle posa sur moi son regard de biche, et me dit : « Appelez-moi donc Yvonne. »

Je fus troublé. « Quel joli prénom », ne puis-je m'empêcher de dire.

« Et vous ? » demanda-t-elle.

« Je m'appelle Augustin, Augustin Meaulnes pour vous servir. »

« On vous appellera Tintin, c'est plus facile à retenir pour les enfaons. »

La courageuse veuve trouvait encore le courage de plaisanter.

Comme le jour déclinait et que la nuit allait bientôt étendre sur la forêt son manteau de velours pailleté d'étoiles d'argent, elle me proposa de passer la nuit chez eux.

Je me demandai si c'était bien correct, le jour même de la mort de son mari. Je lui en fis la remarque, elle me rassura immédiatement : « En tout bien tout honneur », dit-elle.

Les bichons, qui sautillonnaient autour de moi, répétaient : « Reste avec nous Tintin, reste avec nous Tintin. » Ils finirent par me convaincre.

---

* Augustin est toujours nul en orthographe.

*Je l'ai aidée à préparer le repas des petits.
Nous avons épluché des haricots verts, leur
plat préféré, qu'elle sert sans steak haché.
Elle est férocement végétarienne.*

*Elle prétend que si les mamans loups
donnaient plus de haricots verts à leurs
louveteaux, ils n'auraient plus envie de
viande et ils ne deviendraient pas carni-
vores. Les forêts seraient plus sûres et le
Petit Chaperon rouge aurait pu devenir
centenaire.*

*La nuit ne fut pas très bonne, je fus
piqué par les moustiques.*

*Le lendemain, j'aidai la biche pour les
formalités. Comme il est difficile, avec un
sabot, de tenir un porte-plume, je rédigeai
moi-même le texte du faire-part de décès.
Nous décidâmes d'un commun accord de
ne pas en envoyer aux chasseurs.*

*Dans la journée, un personnage très
vieille France a demandé à voir Yvonne.
Il s'agissait d'un chasseur, un de ceux qui
avaient tué son cerf. Il venait présenter ses
condoléances.*

*Comme quoi les chasseurs ne sont pas
tous des gros cons, certains ont du savoir-
vivre... et du cœur...*

*Je sentais chez elle une véritable inquié-
tude au sujet de l'éducation de ses enfants.*

Elle ne cessait de répéter : « Ils n'ont plus de père, que vont-ils devenir ? Les enfaons ont besoin de l'autorité d'un père, sinon ils tournent mal et plus tard ils brûlent des diligences. »

Puis, sans façon, elle posa sa tête tiède sur mon épaule et me dit : « Souvenez-vous Tintin, hier, quand nous nous sommes vus, vous m'avez dit : "Que puis-je faire pour vous ?" Je n'ai pas répondu, j'étais trop émue. Maintenant je sais vous répondre : adoptez mes faons. »

La décision était difficile à prendre, je suis encore jeune, c'est une responsabilité énorme d'élever des enfaons, surtout ceux des autres.

J'acceptai néanmoins et le lui dis. Folle de joie et très primesautière elle plaqua alors son mufle humide sur ma bouche en feu. Ce fut comme le paradis. Une musique éclata dans le ciel, c'était comme si Richard Clayderman, André Rieux et Bocelli s'étaient unis pour fêter l'événement. J'étais embrasé de partout. Mon petit robinet était aussi de la fête, il se sentit tout à coup à l'étroit dans mon caleçon trop large.

Vous savez tout maintenant, cher docteur. Je viens de prendre un engagement solennel et grave et je compte sur vous pour m'aider à le respecter. J'ai maintenant charge d'âme, mais ma situation actuelle ne me permet pas de subvenir aux besoins de ma nouvelle famille. Aussi, j'ai une requête à vous présenter. Auriez-vous l'obligeance de nous loger, le temps que je trouve une solution ?

Dans l'attente d'une réponse favorable, je vous prie de croire, cher docteur, à mes sentiments filiaux.

Vôtre, Augustin MEAULNES.

À la fin de l'histoire, le médecin avait les larmes aux yeux.

Il décide d'aider Augustin et ouvre les portes de son établissement. Ce qui ne sera pas sans poser quelques problèmes.

Pendant la nuit, la biche Yvonne a mangé le rosier de la cour d'honneur.

La pelouse est dans un état innommable. Pelée, remplie de trous, elle est couverte de crottes de biche.

Hier on a retrouvé un faon à l'infirmerie, il dormait sur la table d'examen.

Augustin refuse de manger de la viande, il ne veut que de la verdure. La seule vue d'un bifsteck lui met les larmes aux yeux.
Il broute parfois la pelouse.
Il passe ses journées à batifoler sur la pelouse avec la biche et ses petits faons.

Le médecin chef trouve l'état d'Augustin préoccupant. Il a beaucoup changé, il ne se lave plus, il ne se rase plus, il a le visage couvert de poils, il refuse de mettre des chaussures, il circule pieds nus et il a de plus en plus une forte odeur de gibier.

Les visites ont été interdites. Il ne faut pas que sa mère le voie dans cet état. Le spectacle peut être fatal à la pauvre femme.

POÈME ÉCRIT
PAR LE GRAND MEAULNES
PENDANT SON SÉJOUR
À L'ASILE DE VIERZON

Je suis ton cerf, cerf, cerf,
Serre-moi, serre-moi fort.
Tâte mes andouillers
Vois comme ils sont durs.
Comme mon andouillette
Et sous les frondaisons, chiche
Faisons des bichons, ma biche.

Mardi 15 mai

Hier, nous sommes passés près d'un drame. La biche Yvonne qui folâtrait dans le parc s'est approchée du bâtiment de la direction. Il n'y avait personne. Elle est entrée dans le hall et elle a vu, accroché au mur au-dessus de la porte, un trophée de chasse, les bois d'un cerf.

Elle a prétendu que c'étaient les andouillers de son mari, elle a eu une crise de nerfs.

On dut faire venir Augustin pour la calmer. Elle n'a rien voulu entendre. Écœurée, elle est partie vomir dans l'étang que le soleil couchant empourpre.

Lundi 28 mai

Le traitement prescrit par le médecin chef pour soigner Augustin et le
convaincre qu'il n'est pas un cerf risque
d'être long.

Après des potions qui n'ont eu aucun
résultat, le médecin a entrepris une psy-
chothérapie.

Lors du dernier entretien Augustin a
accepté de répéter plusieurs fois, d'abord
avec le médecin puis tout seul : « Non je
ne suis pas un cerf, je suis un homme. »

Mais avec lui rien n'est jamais définitivement acquis, ainsi qu'en témoigne cette
dernière anecdote.

Le lendemain du jour où Augustin a
reconnu qu'il n'était pas un cerf, le
médecin le voit arriver haletant.

Il se cache sous le bureau. Le médecin
le calme et lui demande la raison de sa

125

frayeur. Augustin prétend qu'il est poursuivi par des chasseurs. Le médecin lui rap-
pelle sa déclaration de la veille : « Vous
savez bien que vous n'êtes pas un cerf, vous
n'avez rien à craindre des chasseurs. »

Augustin fait cette étonnante réponse :
« Moi, je sais maintenant que je ne suis
plus un cerf, mais les chasseurs, est-ce
qu'ils le savent* ? »

---

* Cette formule passera à la postérité. Elle est
couramment utilisée comme chute dans les his-
toires de fou.

Samedi 2 juin

Augustin est guéri, enfin presque. Le médecin a signé le bon de sortie définitif.

Avant le retour à la maison, il a voulu nous voir, ma mère et moi, pour nous donner quelques consignes.

Augustin va mieux mais il est encore faible de la tête, il va falloir faire attention, une rechute est toujours possible.

Le médecin nous a déclaré que les maladies de la tête, comme le romantisme, ne guérissent jamais totalement. Le patient reste fragile.

L'alcool et toutes les boissons alcoolisées sont interdits.

Augustin doit réapprendre à manger de la viande. Commencer par des volailles, il faut lui redonner le goût du blanc de poulet. Au début les viandes seront hachées et mélangées à des légumes.

Pas de gibier tout de suite.

Il serait souhaitable de l'éloigner de la campagne pendant la période de la chasse.

Il ne faut jamais faire allusion à son internement. Il ne faut jamais le laisser rêvasser. Il ne faut pas lui laisser écouter du Chopin et surtout pas de cor de chasse. Remplacer par du Bach.

Il doit pratiquer beaucoup d'activités physiques. Le médecin nous a dit : « Il faut fatiguer la bête. »

Mercredi 6 juin

Augustin est revenu définitivement à la maison. Il a beaucoup changé.

Il a grandi et il a grossi à l'asile. C'est maintenant un colosse.

Il a les cheveux ras. On a dû lui raser la tête, il avait attrapé des poux. Peut-être un cadeau d'Yvonne et de ses bichons.

Il est beaucoup plus calme, à la limite ennuyeux. Parfois je regrette l'Augustin d'avant. Certainement il était méchant mais au moins il était marrant.

Maintenant il passe son temps devant la télévision, à regarder la vie des animaux.

Un an plus tard

Juin 1917

Voilà maintenant une année qu'Augustin est sorti de l'asile. Il mène une vie normale, simplement le médecin lui a donné des gouttes. Il les prend consciencieusement tous les soirs.

Pour savoir si Augustin est définitivement guéri et s'il peut arrêter les gouttes, le médecin a voulu tenter une expérience. Il a demandé à notre mère de le conduire dans le domaine où se trouve, en pension, la biche Yvonne. Pour voir ses réactions.

Nous sommes partis un matin, un peu tendus.

La biche Yvonne, qui n'avait vraisemblablement rien oublié, s'est précipitée au-devant de lui accompagnée de ses jeunes bichettes et de ses daguets.

Elle a bien vieilli, sa silhouette s'est

épaissie et de nombreux poils blancs par-
sèment sa robe.

Comment va réagir Augustin ?

Nous l'observons avec un peu d'inquiétude. Ne va-t-il pas à nouveau se prendre
pour un cerf ?

Il n'a pas un regard pour elle, apparem-
ment il ne l'a pas reconnue. L'expérience
est concluante. En revanche il ne quitte
pas du regard une bichette, certainement
une fille d'Yvonne, qui caracole et lui fait
des yeux de biche.

La biche Yvonne a vu son manège. Elle
sort un mouchoir de son sac et, discrète-
ment, tourne la tête, pour pleurer.

Notre mère dissipe le malaise en décla-
rant : « Il est temps d'aller déjeuner. » Elle
a retenu une table à l'Auberge de la Forêt.

Le repas est agréable, on peut cette fois
dire qu'Augustin est définitivement guéri :
comme plat, il a pris du gigot de biche.

Septembre 1917

Augustin est redevenu méchant, comme avant.

Il me fait encore plus peur maintenant, parce qu'il est plus costaud.

Il a une nouvelle habitude. Au lieu de se battre avec ses poings, il se bat avec sa tête.

Il n'hésite pas à donner des coups de boule, en toute occasion, comme s'il avait des cornes.

15 août 1917

Il fait très lourd. Derrière le ciel de plomb se prépare un orage.

Nous passons près de l'étang malsain. Le vent qui remue les saules est tiède. Quoiqu'en sueur, je ne suis pas très chaud pour me baigner. Augustin y tient au contraire, il insiste pour que je me baigne avec lui.

Il me récite un petit poème de sa composition.

« *L'onde est fraîche, viens donc faire trempette à ton andouillette...* »

Il se met en caleçon et se jette dans l'eau. Quand le Grand Meaulnes a une idée dans la tête il ne l'a pas ailleurs, il vaut mieux ne pas le contrarier. Pour avoir la paix, je cède.

Augustin veut m'entraîner au milieu de l'étang, là où l'eau est épaisse et noire. Je ne veux pas y aller. Je nage très moyennement et, prudent, je reste toujours là où j'ai pied.

Augustin me fait des grands signes avec les bras, il prétend que là où il est, il a pied. Je finis par le rejoindre. Je n'ai plus pied, il m'a menti. Je suis pris de panique, je me débats, je remue mes bras et mes jambes de façon désordonnée.

Augustin s'approche de moi avec une expression étrange, ses yeux jettent des éclairs noirs, il met ses mains sur mes épaules et pèse de tout son poids.

Je m'enfonce...

Samedi 16 août, le matin

J'ouvre les yeux, je suis couché dans notre chambre. Maman est à mes côtés avec le docteur, Augustin me regarde, l'air faussement attristé.

Maman est grave. « Tu peux dire merci à ton frère. Sans lui, mon pauvre enfant, tu ne serais plus de ce monde. »

Je ne comprends pas bien tout de suite. Je regarde Augustin, il a son expression faux cul. La lumière se fait dans mon esprit. Non seulement il a voulu me noyer, mais il a convaincu notre mère qu'il m'avait sauvé. Elle croit toujours ce qu'il raconte.

Notre mère raccompagne le médecin. Augustin reste dans la chambre, il s'approche du lit, il me pince très fort le bras à travers les draps et me dit : « Tu ne perds rien pour attendre. » Il sort.

Mon propre frère souhaite ma mort. J'ai peur.

Il va recommencer, il va trouver quelque chose. Il finira bien par réussir. Déjà, à deux ans, il voulait me tuer avec une casserole.

Je suis en danger, ma vie va devenir un cauchemar, je ne vais plus oser dormir dans la même chambre qu'Augustin, il va essayer de m'étouffer pendant mon sommeil.

Qu'est-ce que je peux faire ? Je n'ai personne à qui me confier. Je me vois mal dire à ma mère : « Maman, Augustin veut me tuer. » Elle me donnerait une gifle en me disant : « Antoine, tu es un gros ingrat. »

Samedi 30 août 1917

Hier j'ai failli mourir.

Augustin avait mis des petits morceaux de verre dans mon bol de lait.

Heureusement, avant de boire, grâce à un rayon de soleil, je les ai vus briller.

Il faut que je parte avant qu'il ne soit trop tard.

Dimanche 31 août, le matin

Je me suis sauvé dans la nuit, c'est mieux pour tout le monde.

On dira : le Petit Meaulnes a disparu.

Je suis sûr qu'on ne préviendra même pas les gendarmes.

De peur qu'on me retrouve.

Trente ans après...

Août 1947

Je viens de recevoir un télégramme d'Augustin. Notre mère est morte.

Toute l'enfance, que je croyais définitivement enfouie, remonte à la surface, comme la boue au fond d'un étang malsain.

J'avais juré de disparaître définitivement, aujourd'hui j'ai envie de retourner là-bas, pour voir.

Qu'est-ce que je vais retrouver ? Est-ce qu'Augustin a toujours envie que je disparaisse ? Certainement pas. Maintenant qu'il a réussi, il n'a plus rien à craindre de moi.

Le village n'a pas changé, la maison non plus.

Des gens habillés en noir, graves et silencieux, avec parfois un bouquet de fleurs, entrent et sortent. Je me mêle aux visiteurs, je pénètre dans la maison. Personne ne me reconnaît.

Je retrouve le papier peint du couloir avec ses grosses fleurs, le tableau avec une vue des Alpes.

Devant le cercueil, une nuque épaisse et moite qui déborde d'un col glacé. Plus haut, un crâne fort dégarni.

Soudain le crâne se retourne. Un visage de notable de campagne apparaît en gros plan, Augustin.

Le Grand Meaulnes est chauve. Le Grand Meaulnes a des bajoues. Le Grand Meaulnes a une dent en or. Le Grand

Meaulnes a le regard éteint, les paupières molles. Le Grand Meaulnes a un costume trois pièces. Le Grand Meaulnes est bedonnant.

Une petite femme boulotte, en noir, lui parle à l'oreille, certainement sa femme, celle à qui il doit dire ma biche.

Le gros Meaulnes m'a reconnu. Il s'approche, il me prend dans ses bras. Il sent l'alcool, il me serre à m'étouffer, je sens son gros ventre mou. Il me lâche enfin. Sauvé.

Il pleure, moi pas. C'est terrible, j'ai plutôt envie de rire.

Une fois encore, il aurait gagné au test du buvard. Où a-t-il caché son oignon ?

Le lendemain

L'enterrement a été vite expédié.

Après la cérémonie Augustin a voulu que je l'accompagne chez lui.

Sa maison est moderne, cossue. Sur la plaque de cuivre gravée, on peut lire « AUGUSTIN MEAULNES ASSURANCES TOUTES BRANCHES. »

Le Grand Meaulnes n'aime plus les risques. Il est définitivement guéri de son romantisme. Lui qui rêvait du grand bonheur, maintenant il se contente de peu.

La salle à manger en merisier massif, est massive. Dans le salon, le canapé et les fauteuils sont en cuir pleine peau. Il y a des petites tables en tutu, couvertes de bibelots mignards. Sur le papier peint façon velours de Gênes, sont accrochés des tableaux pas très beaux, la tapisserie de la dame à la licorne, des glaces dorées à l'or fin, des casseroles en cuivre, des trophées de chasse.

Ça brille et c'est moche.

Sa femme, qu'il appelle Yvonne, est une très bonne ménagère mais elle a un goût de chiottes.

Augustin s'en fout, il s'occupe de ses affaires, de sa cave, de ses fusils.

Il a pris sur le tard la passion de la chasse. Chaque dimanche il va assassiner quelques cervidés, histoire de régler des comptes avec sa jeunesse.

Il a une fille, une survivante des oreillons du papa. Elle est lourde et pâle, comme une endive, elle ressemble à son père. Ils l'ont appelée Ophélie. Elle fait des études dans une école de commerce.

Le repas est banal et long. Augustin a la délicatesse de me proposer le blanc du poulet. Il parle beaucoup, de lui surtout. Il ne demande même pas ce que je fais, ce que je deviens.

Après le repas, les alcools et les cigares. Sa femme veut l'en empêcher, ce n'est pas bon pour lui, le médecin le lui a interdit. Il a eu un accident cardiaque. Il a failli mourir à cause d'un tuyau bouché. Le comble pour celui qui voulait toujours déboucher les éviers.

Il se ressert un verre d'eau-de-vie de prune. Il décide une petite promenade, pour revoir les lieux de notre enfance.

Nous sommes retournés à la maison. Il a ouvert le piano, j'ai peur qu'il se mette à jouer. Il a dû le sentir, il l'a refermé tout de suite.

Notre chambre est toujours pareille, avec nos deux lits. Je revois Augustin en caleçon en train de me réciter un poème.

Maintenant qu'il est riche, il doit porter des slips Kangourou. Et son petit robinet, est-ce qu'il a grandi ? Il ne doit plus le voir à cause de son gros ventre.

Est-ce qu'il s'en sert encore ? Il m'a dit qu'il avait une maîtresse, elle s'appelle Valentine.

Notre mère avait gardé le coffre à jouets, j'ai revu mon ours borgne et sa biche sans queue.

Augustin veut bien s'occuper de vendre

la maison, il gardera les meubles pour se dédommager de sa peine.

Il a voulu me faire monter en haut du village pour contempler son domaine. Il m'a montré tous ses terrains. Il les a achetés à bon prix, c'étaient des terrains agricoles. Comme il est maire, il a beaucoup de relations en haut lieu, il va les revendre comme terrain à bâtir, dix fois plus cher.

Il a surtout un grand projet, l'œuvre de sa vie, c'est sa fille Ophélie qui en a eu l'idée. Ils vont créer ensemble une chaîne de magasins qui s'appellera « AU GRAND MEAULNES ». Des magasins de vêtements pour homme, comme « AU PIGEON VOYA-GEUR », « AU SOLDAT LABOUREUR », en plus chic.

L'affaire se présente bien. Ophélie a contacté des banquiers, des fabricants, des couturiers. Tous ont l'air enthousiastes. Ils trouvent le nom « Grand Meaulnes » très porteur.

Il s'agira d'une collection de vêtements haut de gamme, sport mais chic, style gentle-man-farmer, avec des étoffes nobles, des velours, des tweeds anglais... toujours avec une touche romantique.

152

« Qu'est-ce que tu en penses ? » me demande-t-il.

Je n'en pense rien. Là où on en est... Alors Augustin rame, il fait de la surenchère, il me fait des propositions : « Si ça marche, on va avoir besoin de monde. Tu pourras venir travailler avec nous, faire la comptabilité, toi qui as toujours été fort en maths. De toute façon, on en reparlera, j'ai besoin de ta signature pour l'utilisation commerciale du nom Meaulnes. Tu es d'accord bien sûr ? » Il m'a demandé ça avec un gras sourire d'épicier.

Je n'écoute plus ce qu'il dit. Je pars en avant, j'ai la nausée.

Nous passons le long de l'étang malsain. Est-ce qu'il se souvient ?

Moi, très bien.

Augustin a en projet une résidence au bord de l'étang, il va faire couper tous les saules. Il l'appellera « la Résidence des Saules », en mémoire des saules.

On est très près de l'eau, il faut faire attention, le chemin est boueux et glissant.

Il me suit en soufflant, il ne doit plus savoir nager, surtout avec tout ce qu'il a bu à table, avec son costume trois pièces et son lourd manteau en cuir...

Je le pousse dans l'étang.

J'entends derrière moi un gros plouf,

des gargouillis, des glouglous, des cla-
potis.

Puis plus rien.

Je pars sans me retourner, léger. Maman
ne peut plus me punir.

Le corps fut retrouvé quelques jours plus tard par un pêcheur. Il flottait à la surface, le ventre à l'air comme un poisson mort. Énorme et tout gonflé d'eau.

Il est plus gros mort que vivant, le Grand Meaulnes.

Dans la grosse tête du Grand Meaulnes on a trouvé :

Un buste de Frédéric Chopin
Un poème de Henri de Régnier
Un costume de dandy romantique
Un lutrin
Une lanterne vénitienne
Un luth aux cordes cassées
Un candélabre
Une armure du Moyen Âge
Un glaive
Une plume de paon
Une biche empaillée
Un Pierrot blafard
Un pot de vaseline

Un coffret d'acajou rempli de fiente de pigeon séchée

Un flacon de cristal rempli de larmes

Et quelques oignons pour pleurer quand il n'y a pas de raison...

Table

Avis au lecteur   9

Journal du Petit Meaulnes   15
La disparition d'Augustin   83
Un an plus tard   131
Trente ans après... 143

Du même auteur :

Grammaire française et impertinente, Payot, 1992
Arithmétique appliquée et impertinente, Payot, 1993
Le Pense-Bêtes de saint François d'Assise, Le Pré-aux-
    Clers, 1983 ; Payot, 1994
Peinture à l'huile et au vinaigre, Payot, 1994
Le Curriculum vitae de Dieu, Seuil, 1995
Le Pain des Français, Seuil, 1996
Sciences naturelles et impertinentes, Payot, 1996
Je vais t'apprendre la politesse, p'tit con, Payot, 1998
Il a jamais tué personne, mon papa, Stock, 1999
La Noiraude, Encore la Noiraude, Pas folle la Noiraude,
    Stock, 1999/2000/2001
Roulez jeunesse, Payot, 2000
J'irai pas en enfer, Stock, 2001
Mouchons nos morveux, Lattès, 2002

Composition réalisée par IGS-CP

IMPRIMÉ EN ESPAGNE PAR LIBERDUPLEX
Barcelone
Dépôt légal éditeur : 49337-09/2004
Édition 01
LIBRAIRIE GÉNÉRALE FRANÇAISE – 31, rue de Fleurus – 75006 Paris

ISBN : 2-253-10960-6   31/0960/0